Outside
      Shooter

SPORTS AND AMERICAN CULTURE SERIES
BRUCE CLAYTON, EDITOR

# Outside
# Shooter

*A Memoir*

# Philip Raisor

UNIVERSITY OF MISSOURI PRESS   COLUMBIA AND LONDON

Copyright © 2003 by
The Curators of the University of Missouri
University of Missouri Press, Columbia, Missouri 65201
Printed and bound in the United States of America
All rights reserved
5  4  3  2  1     07  06  05  04  03

Library of Congress Cataloging-in-Publication Data

Raisor, Philip, 1938–
     Outside shooter : a memoir / Philip Raisor.
            p. cm. — (Sports and American culture series)
Includes bibliographical references and index.
     ISBN 0-8262-1484-3 (pbk. : alk. paper)
     ISBN 0-8262-1508-4 (alk. paper)
  1. Raisor, Phillip, 1938–  2. Basketball players—United
States—Biography.  I. Title.  II. Series.
     GV884.R325A3 2003
     796.323'092—dc21
                                                  2003006705

∞™ This paper meets the requirements of the
American National Standard for Permanence of Paper
for Printed Library Materials, Z39.48, 1984.

Text design: Stephanie Foley
Cover design: Kristie Lee
Typesetter: Foley Design
Printer and binder: Thomson-Shore, Inc.
Typeface: ITC Korinna

for FLOYD and CATHERINE

*parents and friends*
*alive and alert*
*at ninety-seven*
*a blessing for generations*

# Contents

In order to be aware that you are looking at a basketball, it is not enough for the basketball to be represented as a purely visual pattern (a round, orange object with thin black lines around it) by your visual system. The pattern has to also have grabbed the attention of the working memory.

—JOSEPH LEDOUX,
*The Emotional Brain*

We live forward,
 we understand backward.

—THOMAS HARDY
 *quoting* WILLIAM JAMES
 *quoting* SØREN KIERKEGAARD

# Outside
## Shooter

# Defeat Begins Inside

"They're already calling this the game of the century."

—*Hoosiers*

As a starting guard on the Muncie Bearcats, and with our team headed for the 1954 state championship basketball tournament in Indianapolis, I had to be careful. No twisted ankle for me, not now. My first steps off the back porch into the March snow were hesitant, my high-tops sniffing for a mole hole or stump. I tucked my gym bag in my letter jacket so both hands would be free, and I waddled through our backyard, past a single hoop with a frayed net on an ancient backboard. When I got to the garbage truck tracks in the alley, I could shuffle faster, and hearing old man Jennings' Doberman, I tried to run, but slipping, almost falling, I clutched the air and a prayer and found myself sliding on smooth ice. The rhythm was fine and I started dribbling my imaginary ball past garages and firing at imaginary rims. I didn't miss a shot. I knew I was ready. The bridge over White River had been plowed clean, cars streamed over it, arms waving at me as I passed and the voices like trumpets in a Hollywood movie—"Go get 'em, buddy! Beat 'em, pal!" I almost fast-breaked to the charter bus parked at the Field House; purple and white signs and streamers blazoned its sides: "Go Bearcats." "Beat Elkhart. Beat Milan."

My teammates—Flowers, Hinds, Jimmy, Big John, and the rest—were already there, and surrounding us were the cheering block, majorettes, and nine hundred fans who had just learned that Joe Turner's new release, "Shake, Rattle And Roll," could be played as loud as car radios would allow. The band bus joined us, and accompanied by tubas, cymbals, and a drummer banging on the roof of a '48 Chevy, we headed out of town like a chain of animals obeying a performance command. Our caravan was going to Butler Field House, and all around Indiana similar masses were clogging rural roads and state highways. Milan, Elkhart, Muncie, and Terre Haute were sending their prized teams to a single-division tournament where any school, no matter the size, could claim the annual trophy.

With our bus rumbling down Highway 67, Coach McCreary, standing in the aisle, his Irish redness flush and sweating, created the image he wanted us to share. We were rockets in a cannon: "That's a circus outside," he insisted. "But we're inside. We're poised and deadly, and we're going to blow some bodies away."

I was a fifteen-year-old whose community and family tradition made it impossible not to be at least a bullet.

Muncie, Indiana, has been sociology's dream. A small city (forty thousand in 1924; sixty-seven thousand in 2000), Muncie was the first American community whose total culture was examined with scientific detachment. *Middletown* (1929), by Robert and Helen Lynd, set the standard for future studies, both of Muncie and numerous other cities in America. Three replications (1937, 1982, 1983), memoirs, histories, photographic collections, and a six-part PBS series have cracked open the chest of this town.

Inside? The whole system of social change. Diagnosis? Little has changed.

After the failure of the natural-gas boom of the late nineteenth century ended its dream of becoming an industrial center, Muncie hunkered down and sought a "psychological solidarity" that would protect it from unsettling invasions. But "we don't want you coming in" really means "come ahead." Combative and defensive, Muncie built its own history, stealing only what it needed from the world's to make sense of itself. Whatever the divisions within class, race, and family, they were not sufficient to undermine conformity with local customs. Said one social scientist, after studying Muncie, "This city in the American heartland bears a strange resemblance to a tribal society in New Guinea or central Africa." Athletics was one of the principal activities which preserved that vision. On Friday nights a basketball or football game was played, and all over the county—on radios in bars, homes, and drive-in parking lots—a win or loss, a heroic play, or some silly coach's decision would bond the community like an aboriginal chant.

My father and brother were my models. They had to be. Anyone would have said I was a fool to look elsewhere. In junior high school I would go with them to the Field House to sell Christmas trees for Kiwanis. All evening I would see them, surrounded by old men and young boys alike, talking about basketball. The old men would remember when my father played on the 1923 team that fell one game short of winning the state championship and then eight years later when he was the assistant coach for the team that did win the state title. The young boys would ask my brother what it was like to be on *two* state championship teams (1951 and 1952) and whether he thought we'd ever win another. "You've got big shoes to fill," I would hear enough times to be pleased, intimidated, and nauseated.

But overt pressure did not come from my father or brother, nor from the scrapbooks my mother meticulously and gleefully maintained. It came from seeing just how integral athletic success was in the whole fabric of our family. Growing up, I would tag along with my brother, three years older than I, to the tennis court for lessons, the baseball field for shortstop practice, and the playground for the citywide summer night games where sharp elbows were the rule. He'd thrust me in the midst of older and larger players, and then defend me when I was not quite tough enough to hold my own. Athletics was our way— as it was for many families in Muncie—to preserve what we did not want changed.

City and family supporting me, a history of challenge and nurture, I should have been sitting on that bus begging the fuse to be lit. And I was, for a while.

Coach McCreary continued to work us, firmly clutching our shoulders or roughing our hair or smacking Jimmy on the butt when he leaned out the window, pumping his fist. But I was never very good at waiting, of using time patiently to build resolve. Give me a half hour of sitting, and I would be all over the place: *Beekeeping. That sounds like a good hobby. How do I start without getting stung from tail to toe? What kind of hive do I get? What kind of bees?* Or I would think: *I'm Holden Caulfield* of Catcher in the Rye *walking down Forty-fifth Street—phoney adults, always thinking of themselves. Just depresses you to death.* I found myself looking at the back of Gene Flowers' broad neck and thinking that Wayne Klepfer's fist must have been that size when it smashed into my face at an ice-cream social.

Wayne was as large as his brother (an all-state wrestling champion) with a Mack truck attitude. The previous spring, with a hundred people not watching, he had walked up to me, said he didn't like my looks, and busted me. I guess, as someone later explained, I had elbowed him in a ninth-grade basketball game. Then a hundred people did watch as I swung back instinctively and caught him coming in for the kill. I had bought a big squared ring at the Delaware County Fair a week before, and it broke his nose. Blood sprayed on Mr. Zedekar, the principal, and Wayne and I were immediately separated and banished. I heard very quickly that he and his brother were prowling the neighborhood for me. Later again, I learned that just the week before, Wayne had broken a fellow's jaw into a hundred fragments, and all summer long I imagined my face splayed like a kaleidoscope if he caught me. The fear was intrusive, burrowing, and it settled in and took charge.

Such a fear doesn't fill up blood and bones; it leaves a hole. I found myself comfortable only in dark and shadows. All my arguments against myself, my cowardice, my unwillingness to stray far from my backyard basketball court, were swallowed by a big black mouth in my stomach. I started my sophomore year walking into Central High expecting that Wayne Klepfer and his southside gang would be waiting in the hallway, or just around the corner.

After the first month of basketball season, I landed on the starting team of the Muncie Bearcats. Jimmy Barnes (5' 8") and I (5' 10") were elevated from the B team to the A team when, after two losses, Coach McCreary called for a radical change. He had height on the front line: Hines (6' 4"), Flowers (6' 3"), and Casterlow (6' 6"), but he wanted speed and quickness. Throughout the rest of the season we won most of the games and entered the sectional tournament ranked fourth in the state with a 23-5 record.

Yet we struggled to become what at every practice we were instructed to become, a unit. "Act as one unit!" Coach would shout. "How you going to roll over anybody if you're not a tank!" World War II and, particularly, the Korean War were recent history, and even in "quiet" blue-collar Muncie military metaphors were popular ways to divide or conquer. Playgrounds, basketball courts, drive-ins became "battlegrounds" and "ground zero," and anyone who would toss up garbage shots would get blown up like a bridge. Jimmy and I were newcomers, the recruits, and we knew the lieutenants and colonel who framed the tactics. Among ourselves, our hierarchy worked, and although we did not hang together off court, we did not find the northside/southside divisions or the black/white tensions in the community divisive, though the team members were predominantly southside and white. Our trash talk was wit not war, a relaxing shower ritual:

"Hey, white boy. You're a clammy lookin' piece a shell."

"Yeah, Big John, well black is the color of my true love's hair and, by the way, what is the color of your momma?"

"Yeah, un-huh. And I'll blow you up like a bridge."

"You keep strokin' your plunger you blow your own self up."

But all is not what it seems. If timing and balance fail, the "perfect" circus act collapses. John Casterlow walked on a high wire. He would joke and jaw, but also smash a door or face. We learned that he was quick-witted and quick-fisted. That was John. We lived with it, feeling secure he had it fine-tuned. He was our enforcer, rule breaker, and, I thought, my buddy. He was black and southside; I was white and northside.

But again, the balance, the balance.

One night on a road trip to South Bend, John led us past one of Coach's unenforceable rules: stay in your room. Who could? The snow was coming down in white furrows. It settled on hills, in gullies, and turned the parking lot into a no-man's land. Gene Flowers, our all-state halfback, fired a round of snowballs at "Duke" Scott, who took no crap from nobody, and the range war was on. I clipped John with a grenade and he was all over me, laughing as he packed me in snow and slowly rolled me

down a hill. Then I heard what he heard from one of the motel
windows. "Just some niggers being niggers." I don't know why
John grabbed harder, but I felt his hands shake me and then
wrench my testicles. His face grew angry and distant; he spit
in the snow and rubbed my face in it, pressing harder into my
groin. I tried to cry out but could only cry. This was not play;
this was rage. It was what I had feared in Wayne Klepfer—urgent,
desperate revenge. Then John stopped (Did he hear my begging? Did he get where he was going?). He stared at me with
absolutely no emotion and walked back toward his room. We
won again that night. But John, a prolific scorer, had no points
and committed three hard fouls in the first quarter.

Jimmy Angelopolous, *Indianapolis Times* sportswriter, set
the media tone for the state finals tournament: "Think of the
rich heritage of Indiana tournament lore and you think of Muncie
Central's Bearcats. Think of Indiana's greatest in basketball
and you can't forget Muncie Central and Coach Jay McCreary.
Think of Indiana's 1954 high school basketball championships
in Indianapolis Saturday and everyone had better remember
Muncie and McCreary. They're cut from the same bolt of cloth.
Individually or collectively, they've woven the fabric of basketball since 1928. Today—26 years later—they're threading their
way toward an unprecedented fifth state prep championship."
Heady stuff for a fifteen-year-old, but I could feign confidence, even cockiness, as well as anyone. When I stepped off
the bus on Saturday, a reporter, microphone at our mouths,
eased with me through the crowd toward Butler Field House.
He said he'd heard a story about me—that before one game
in American Legion baseball, a teammate had been juking a
bat in my face, back-and-forth, back-and-forth, and accidentally let it slip; it smashed into my face, busted three teeth into
pieces; I stuffed a handkerchief in my mouth, the story goes,
and insisted on playing. Was it true I pitched a no-hitter and
had four hits? "No," I'd said, reaching down to sign an auto-
graph for a little girl in saddle shoes and pleated skirt. "It was
only three." The story straight now, "Tough kid," he said and
walked away. I remember that Casterlow, arm around my
shoulders and laughing, shook his head. "Ain't you one big

Mr. Atlas." He was healed now. We were OK. John was still being John.

The saddle shoes were everywhere. Kicked high by cheer-leaders, painted differently by fan clubs, and tossed to the side by jitterbuggers, the saddles starred on a stage of colliding colors and sounds. From buses to the cavernous interior of Butler Field House, yellow, purple, green ties dangled below creped derbies or Indian feathers. Terre Haute had its Black Cats prowling in full gear or pinned to lapels. A whole section of Elkhart's Blue Blazers sang the school's song outside and then, packed close, streaked to their seats. "Watch out! Watch out!" someone shouted, and an enormous purple and white yo-yo dropped from a second tier window and rolled through the crowd. As we entered the locker room, we could hear behind us the squawking of a parrot: "Kick Muncie's ass! Kick Muncie's ass!"

We knew the parrot's sentiment was shared by three-fourths of the crowd of fifteen thousand and by most of the basketball followers in the state. We had won too often. Our response was so Muncie-like. We hunkered down and thrust our chests to the world. A chant against us was another brick in the barricade. Jim Hinds was often a wall of silence, but his expressions were verbal and pointed. His eyes especially said you were a jerk or let me tell you this dirty joke. Before the afternoon game he sat on a turned-over trash basket and soaked his forever-swollen knees. At times he could barely walk, and when he played he ran and jumped stiff legged. As the trainer soaked then taped then braced his knees, Jim sat and "told" us there was no pain, there would be no excuses.

We beat Elkhart by nine points. Our fast break worked like a zipper. Jim and Gene muscled, trapped, and tripped Ray Ball and Ron Stork until the backboards were open pantries, and grabbing quickly, they passed the sweet ball out to Jimmy or me, and we all ran like we had just stolen from grandma. Usually a playmaker, I scored thirteen points, and leaving the floor with the Bearcat fight song sounding louder than I'd ever heard it, I came up behind Jim, his left hand on a wall, his right leg dangling. I offered myself as a brace, and then caught his eyes. "What?" I said. "What's wrong?" He looked away. I felt dismissed. Then he turned back and said, "Pass me the fucking ball."

Milan beat Terre Haute by twelve points. The night game was set—Milan vs. Muncie for the championship. We left the arena for the hotel, rest, and food, leaving behind milling crowds and scalpers. My parents had a room on the second floor, and Coach let me stop by before we headed off for the pregame fare of cold roast beef, warm milk, and something green and stringy. My father was a jittery, joyful mess. "Calm down, Floyd," my mother said, but Dad was replaying the scissors move off Casterlow that got me the jumper and then the rear-turn that set me open for the two-handed set shot. "Just like we did it, boy," he said, and both my mother and I knew where he was going.

He was back in the 1923 season when, having been pro- moted to back guard from the Midget (YMCA) team where he had won all-state honors, he, along with Tooti Thornburg, Art Beckner, Paul Harrold, and Ted Bebout, led the "prayin'-fight- in'" Bearcats to the finals at the Indianapolis Coliseum. The school yearbook called "Toyd" Raisor "one of the flashiest players that ever bore the colors of this school," and the hyper- bole pleased him. His role was to stay behind the center line as the primary defender against a fast break. But he would shoot occasionally, once dropping in a shot a full three quarters the length of the floor. Winning and character he said were what he was taught by the coaches. Prayin' was for the character (they never prayed to win; they prayed that no one got hurt), and confidence was for the fightin'. "We lost that one, son, to Vincennes 27-18, but we got it back in '31, your brother got it back in '51 and '52, and now you've got a chance. Losin' tonight, son, will hurt you all your life."

My mother's calming words for us were simple: "We'll still all be together tomorrow." As I left, I understood what my father was saying; he had been where the "hole" is. He was just say- ing that he had been where the hole is.

Muncie's fifth state crown. Being the only family to have three members playing in a state championship game. Completing my father's dream. My own rookie glory. These were the plus- es I scanned as I walked through the hotel hallway toward my room. Just as I started on the negatives, I saw John slip out of the No Exit door. He turned when I caught up with him on the stairwell; his face was a black wet rag. The thought of John crying was impossible. He accepted my hand on his arm and my gesture to sit on the cement steps. "My mother," he started, then stopped, weighing whether we were close enough for this. I gathered that for the moment he thought we were. "My mother died ten days ago. She won't be here." How did I not know, for God's sake? "John," I started, but he stood, as though relieved or had said enough, I couldn't tell. I simply followed him toward the elevator. The long hall, soft carpet, even the dim lights muted our breathing. Until we heard voices. I looked around the corner and saw a gaggle of Muncie Boosters in purple and white jackets, shoes, hunting caps. We held back.

"They'll all be back next year. Hinds, Flowers, Casterlow, Raisor, Barnes. We win tonight and, great God! we'll win two States in a row."

"Yeah. But there's Crispus Attucks next year. And that's Oscar Robertson. They'll be one tough bunch of coons."

"But remember, old bones. They're all black. You put five of them together on the same floor, and they'll be wandering around looking for a cotton field."

I would have busted into them with John if he'd lifted one foot. He looked at his hands, and then went so deep inside himself it was five minutes before he moved. I can only guess, but combined with his mother's death and this dramatic reminder of his isolation—at this moment, on the verge of such great success—John must have frozen in a sense of doom.

I think I know *now* how long and how thoroughly John had been prepared for this response. Growing up, I never heard "nigger" said in my family or among my friends, until junior high (my elementary had been all white) when my world of friends broadened. Except for an old friend, Charlie, a yard man, I had little contact with black people. My education into the "real" world of race relations, beyond just sensing differences, began when I saw blacks and whites divide in the auditorium at lunch time and when any fight between a black and white student polarized the gathering crowd along racial lines. What I didn't sense or know at that age was that black athletes—hugged when we won, forgiven when we lost—had only one identity at the drive-ins, dances, or downtown: black.

What I was learning in that hotel hallway, reinforced over the next few years, was that in Muncie John had no chance. Forty years later, Gregory Howard Williams in his book, *Life on the Color Line,* about growing up black in Muncie during the fifties and sixties, confirmed this. To Williams, John was a "god," who "soared high above the rim and snatched the ball almost from the top of the backboard," and on one occasion came down to earth to defend Williams against a neighborhood bully. But even black heroes were targets in Muncie. What happened to Williams may have happened to John.

A few years after John graduated, Williams became a Bearcat letter winner. One night, as Williams tells it, he and three friends walked by a local drive-in and as they passed the parking lot they heard the chant of "nigger, nigger." Turning to the crowd, Williams saw some of his classmates. The four boys were well-known athletes, and still on that night rocks and beer cans rained down on them. Finally escaping to the house of one of the boys, Williams says, "We sat in his living room most of the night, trying to comprehend the attack. Brian, the star of the basketball team who was receiving scholarship offers from all over the country, said, 'Don't matter what you achieve or how big you get, you'll always be a nigger in Muncie.'"

Milan is in the heel of boot-shaped Indiana and stands leisurely in a checkerboard of alfalfa, corn, and wheat. Like rural towns of a thousand or so people all over America, Milan mixes small business and farming to serve its needs. In 1954, Nichols Barbershop on Carr Street or Chris Volz's garage or Kirschner's Hardware or any one of about forty businesses would collect all the talk that mattered. Large-scale urban growth or racial conflict were not the subjects, but, more often than not, basketball was. Bobby Plump, Ray Craft, Gene White, and most of the Milan Indians, pals since childhood, were known and seen personally almost every day by the townspeople. Open to advice, ribbing, and criticism, the boys were heroes. The 1953 and 1954 teams bonded the community even more than in Muncie; there were no subterranean issues to separate them. The teams went to the Final Four, a feat for very small schools (160 enrolled in Milan High School) unexcelled by any other team in Indiana prep history. Their slow-down type of game fit the size of the players and the style of the town. When warlike tribes attacked them, they shuffled and swirled, set up the checkers, then moved efficiently. Jump. Capture. King.

None of us knew in 1954 that this game would inspire two Indiana natives, David Anspaugh and Angelo Pizzo, to produce, thirty-two years later, the movie *Hoosiers*—their vision of a small town's reaffirmation of its togetherness through the successful struggles of its high school basketball team. In the final sequences of the film, Hickory High (Milan) meets South Bend (Muncie) for the championship. True to the spirit of the original game (though not its tempo), the movie captures, in numerous scenes, the avalanche of Hoosier hysteria.

I remember the noise when we launched through the purple and white ring of streamers onto the playing floor and were met by the debris of basketball—boos, catcalls, armpit squawks. The stomping and yelling of our cheering block countered, and when Milan appeared the clatter accelerated, swept to the top of the dome, and pulled every person there, I'm sure, into the heart of cacophony. No one in this explosion of sounds, smells, and joy could have felt alone.

As we loosened up, drove in for lay-ups, began to feel the sweat and fully realize, yes, we are here, I saw my brother, Tom, walk past our bench. Now playing on the University of Michigan basketball team, he had driven down for the game. He settled into the crowd of ex-Bearcats, wearing their letter jackets, pieces of net pinned to hats, and memories poised to break into the present. His letter had reached me the week before: "The thrill of that first championship is unforgettable and unexplainable. I want, more than anything else, for you to experience it!" I looked toward John, to give him something of what I was feeling, but he was swearing at a ball that had ricocheted off his knee.

The referee whistled the center jump. Ray Craft's aftershave lotion startled me as we circled for the jump ball. Not sweat nor stale uniforms, but cologne from the civilian world. I turned on Craft my hand-to-hand combat stare, a strategy that had unsettled a player or two. But his eyes darted from one team-mate to the next, confirming their unity. He wasn't playing war. Within the next few minutes he faked left twice, I leaped, and he deftly slipped around me for open shots.

"Great God! What are you guys doing?" was a question that surfaced early from the bench, the grandstands, and probably my Uncle Om, his ear tucked to a radio. *Hinds down the left side, ball to Barnes, back to Hinds, Hinds fires from twenty feet, off the rim; Raisor into the middle, drops behind the foul line, blasts away, off the rim; Flowers takes a pass, backs out, launches a long one-hander, off the rim; Raisor to Hinds, back to Raisor, back to Hinds who misses from the corner; Casterlow roams the middle, takes a pass from Raisor, flips it back to Barnes, his rocket clangs off the rim; "Time Out! Time! Get the ball into the middle! Jam it into the middle!" Hinds fakes the base line, drives toward the foul circle, out to Flowers, long one-hander, bang! It's in!; Barnes to Raisor in the backcourt, a long two-handed bomb, off the rim; Barnes' bullet ricochets off Casterlow, Hinds digs it out, his long arching hook's on target; Flowers straight down the middle, charges into Gene White, bodies all over the place. Milan leads 14-11 at the end of the first quarter. Get this—the Bearcats shot only 19 percent. They're in trouble.*

John took no shots, collected one rebound. He walked toward the bench, shoulders slumped, a prisoner in a long line. I watched him pull a towel from a manager, bury his face, and revolve it like he was rubbing his nose against a stone wall. Coach stared at him, then gestured to Bob Crawford to head for the scorer's table. He thumbed John to the end of the bench.

*And now Milan's trying to turn it up a notch, clear the board. Plump hits on a short jumper and it's 19-13 early in the second quarter. Craft slips the ball to White and weaves down the middle, curling back to catch Plump's bounce pass. He holds the ball near the center circle, fakes left, fakes right, holds the ball. Cutter slides out, picks, turns, cuts diagonally toward Truitt. They double in the corner. Plump and Craft trade passes. The circle broadens, forcing the game to the edge. Craft cuts straight down the middle for the score, untouched.*

*Agullana replaces Raisor. White breaks the press with a long pass over Hinds, Cutter blocks Crawford, and with a quick step over the fallen Agullana, Craft cooks for two more. Muncie storms inside for a couple of baskets, but Milan recaptures the rhythm, and slipping in and out, backs the Bearcats against the wall at halftime 23-17.*

In the tunnel between the playing floor and locker room, I stopped to dip a towel in ice. We were behind, I had been benched, and sweat was crusted on my body. I smashed the cooler and walked on alone, rubbing my fist. As I turned toward the Players Only room, I saw Wayne Klepfer pass under an EXIT light. I swear I did. The hall was dim and wide, but I knew his size, shape, and enormous fist. He stalked toward me, his shoulders round like a rope. He was grinning as though he had at last cornered his prey. John walked past me, straight through him, and Wayne disappeared. I leaned against a wall as the sense of emptiness swept through me. In that hollowness, I wanted something. I don't know why, but I wanted Wayne back. Maybe it's like in the last phase of a dream, half-awake, we make the story come out the way we want. I wanted Wayne to charge me and then I would collar him, pull him up, and make him say "Get 'em, Phil. Get 'em for us." Why shouldn't Wayne Klepfer lose himself in my state final game and get on my side. He had dragged me into his world and forced me to know what I didn't want to know—that defeat begins inside. I was lost in there, falling. Standing alone in that tunnel I knew I was dreaming, and dreaming of winning, and then I knew we could lose this game. That was a possibility I had not *felt* before.

Benchwarmers. An uncommon condition for John and me. I know what Coach wanted. Agullana to pick up the defense and me to watch the floor play. Simple enough. We weren't cutting, picking, crashing the boards. We weren't blocking the middle. I'd be back in soon. Milan started its weave, again. Plump to Craft and around we go. Milan's socks looked like those leggings the Japanese soldiers wore in the movies *Sands of Iwo Jima* and *March from Bataan*. I watched Milan's leggings go up and down the floor. Just the leggings. Like birds flitting, maybe dancing, swirling, from limb to limb in a single tree. Ray Craft was a crow—like Croft in *The Naked and the Dead*.

Yeah, mean, nasty Croft. I watched the platoon go up the mountain, and Croft take Roth's bird, squeeze it to death, and throw it away. Then the birds were dead. I listened to the crowd, a wind roaring up and down, through gullies, over ridges. I heard the announcer at the scorer's table next to me calling the play-by-play. He was thin, had a thin tie on, a voice as thin as a skeleton. . . . *Barnes throws a nice pass to Hinds; he hits a beautiful shot from the corner . . . and then the platoon moved up the ravine (How'd it go? Something like . . .) from ridge to ridge up the mountain instinctively knowing where the next ridge was . . . Muncie's beginning to bottle up that middle; Craft into the circle, backs out, over to White, to Truitt. Barnes is right there . . . guns aimed from the top of Mount Anaka; the heat, the absence of air, choking, up the ridges, climbing into the burning sky, "I can't go on, I can't" . . . Plump fires, Agullana rebounds, over to Flowers, takes a long one, he hits it! He hits it! Bearcats only down by two . . . "Get up, you sonofabitch"; the rocks slippery, a few yards, up, slowly up the ridgeline, fatigue at the slowness of it all . . . Milan goes into its slowdown again; Craft over to Plump, back to Cutter, over to Plump, he fires, misses, not having his best night shooting . . . Where is the peak? Is the top near, for god's sake? . . . Barnes into Hinds down low, he hits, he's fouled; Muncie can take the lead for the first time since the opening moment . . . O, for a plateau, just some water . . . Hinds misses, that's it, end of the third quarter, score tied 26-26 . . . sonofabitch, let us rest, let us rest . . .*

Straight across from me, among the Muncie fans, I saw my father applauding, laughing, and my mother's hand on his shoulder gently trying to ease him quiet. Coach McCreary gestured. "Raisor, come here." I knew it, offense time, already feeling the ball in my hands. "Sit there with Casterlow," he said. "Keep him up. We might need him." Looking ahead, I didn't see Coach's eyes or face, but his words wedged into me like heavy armor. "Who's going to keep me up?" I thought, falling back to the bench. Seated, John stared at some picture in his mind. Flowers nudged him, patted his shoulder, and walked by me as though looking for something out of place.

Halfway through the fourth quarter, Milan was behind 28-26.

They continued their slow, patterned play. Then when the usual weaves and picks left Plump near the center circle, he backed up one step, looked at his coach, and cupped the ball to his waist. His teammates, too, stepped back, hands on hips. A crowd almost manic throughout the game, unable to sit, no doubt sensing their role in the outcome, fell silent as though watching the lighting of a Christmas tree. Milan wasn't attacking. They were behind and holding the ball, just holding the ball. How do you win that way? After four minutes, there was a brief flurry and exchange of baskets that left the score 30-30. Then Plump, once again, settled down at his post. Coach waved our players back. Even I knew that Milan had stopped our momentum. Hinds began rubbing his knee. Jimmy, the only one arched in defense, set himself six feet from Plump.

I found my brother in the stands. I knew the frustration and anger on his face was not because I had been sent to the bench. Tom was a coach at heart, and he probably accepted Coach's decision to sit me down. He had also gotten over not playing in the final state championship game two years before. That was Coach McCreary's first year at Central, and he had taken a team of veterans from the previous year's state championship team, changed their game from a slow-down to a fast-break team, and brought them back to the finals. Tom was a designated role player ("the best sixth man in the state," one pundit called him), and he loved it—getting assists, setting up teammates, keeping the intensity at a high level. He was the surprise off the bench. In the afternoon game of the 1952 finals, Tom had sparked the team to the win. He understood surprise, he had told me; it changed emotions, momentum, rhythm. Watching him now, I knew what was bothering him. Milan had surprised us; where was ours?

I felt John's elbow. "Ain't that yo momma," he said, pointing to a spot in the stands. I nodded. "Fine lady," he mumbled. Between games during the sectional and regional tournaments the team would come to our house for the closely monitored rest Coach wanted us to have. My mother would bubble around, poised and laughing, as she placed hot meat loaf on plates and urged everyone to take seconds. She would stand in front of John and they would joke back and forth about the size of the seconds. A passing thought in John's mind, and then he was somewhere else.

I kept glancing down the bench to see when Coach would put me back in, but his legs were crossed, he was leaning back, simply watching ahead. I could not believe I was still sitting there, that John was, that we were out of this thing. My mother, his mother—I knew he was trying to fill a hole, but our spaces were still empty. I tried to catch my brother's anger and make it my own. Coach was an idiot. But it wasn't that easy. Tom was standing now with his teammates from the past, urging defense, their own voices a wall against Cutter and Truitt. I watched my brother and then my father rise past themselves to something outside. But I couldn't get there. I sulked. I would have to ask my father's forgiveness for my failure or accept his understanding, whichever came first. I knew already I would play this game over and over, trying to find some way to be a hero. And there was Bobby Plump standing out there in the middle of the floor like a guy in a raincoat exposing himself. I jumped up. "Move the ball, Plump," I yelled. "Play the damn game." I threw my rock at Goliath. Among colliding yells, it turned into a feather.

With eighteen seconds left, and the score still tied, Milan called time out.

I grabbed a towel and moved into the huddle. "Here, Jimmy. Plump'll take the shot." "I know it," he said, as though he had already framed the moves. Quick feet and hands, Jimmy loved two things: to defend and, with a lead, to dribble out the game with everyone chasing him. John slapped him on the head. "Stick with his white ass," he said. Jimmy stalked back onto the floor.

I knew the announcer next to me was describing Plump passing the ball in, but I didn't hear him. I was watching closely. Craft passed it back and Plump dribbled to the center court. Truitt, on the side, waved his teammates toward him. Amazingly, Truitt, Cutter, Craft, and White formed an honor guard all the way to the left, pacing at a bathroom door. Only Jimmy closed in on Plump. Two pieces left on the center court, two moves possible—a drive or jump shot. Plump drove left, quickstepped to the right; Jimmy stayed with him, left hand low, and cut his drive. Plump went straight up as though a pump had inflated him; he went high, floating, the ball on the tips of his fingers, his arm as relaxed as a soft exhalation. John and I leaped from the bench to block his shot . . .

I was living in Virginia when *Hoosiers* was released in 1986. My father had been sending me clippings for the past year during the making of the movie, and I knew that the names had been changed, Gene Hackman was portraying the Milan coach, and Indiana had been steeped in nostalgia for a whole winter. I hadn't visited that game very much in the past decade or so. But on a Friday afternoon, my wife called from the *Virginian-Pilot* where she was on the staff of business news. She said a colleague had tickets to the opening of the movie at a mall theater. Should we go?

The theater was nearly full, half-lit, and happily noisy. We walked through the lobby, past the large poster over the candy counter: two dirty basketball shoes, one on its side, over the plug line—"It'll Go Straight to Your Heart." I went to get my Dots and popcorn. We sat far closer to the screen than usual—way up front. I protested, complaining that my professorial eyes needed some distance from painful events, but the lights coming down stifled my protests. I settled in and listened to the subsiding chatter. Then, the lights slowly came back up and a stereophonic voice, like the one in the planetarium scene in *Rebel without a Cause,* surround-sounded us all: "Ladies and Gentlemen, welcome to the Norfolk premier of *Hoosiers*—the story about the high school team in Indiana which has captured the imagination of the world. Tonight you will see that movie, and the final championship game which makes it so wonderful. David beats Goliath—a final game based upon a real game played in 1954. Tonight we have one of the players who was actually in that original game. He is here tonight (an audible 'oooh' followed). You saw that poster coming in. Well, here is Phil Raisor who was on the *losing,* the *losing* team on that immortal night."

On that immortal night, I slumped down near the foul circle and waited for things to clear and the postgame ceremonies to begin. Milan's cheering block formed on the floor and our cheerleaders gently stroked us with pom-poms. A few security guards tried to hold back the crowd. I saw the skeleton standing in a mass of color and bodies shouting over the radio, "Can you hear me out there! Can you hear me!" A gnarled Indian face, half-painted, half dripping with sweat and beard, attacked me with an unyielding breath: "Got your ass! Got your ass!" I knew there was no point in trying to find my father's face, or my brother's, but, surprisingly, in that moment of defeat, I knew my mother was right. All things are not as they seem today, or any day. We'd be together tomorrow; the world continues on a level deeper than what we can see.

A black knee nudged me and I looked up at John. His face was calm, his eyes warm with resignation. Six years later he would be killed on a Detroit street. The *Detroit News* reported that John waded into three men who were harassing his eight-een-year-old wife, Annie, and they knifed him and beat him to death with an iron bar. But on this night, John leaned down and said, "We got this to share, man. You and me. We got this to share." I let him help me up, and then, I realized I'd almost missed it. John knew I was in trouble. *He* had been watching me. "Sometimes, little brotha, you got to share your pain to get out of it."

I knew I would remember what he said, and maybe someday understand it. John had been deeper than I had been, but for now I knew no one else could see this game the way we did. We had sat on a hard bleacher for the past hour, roamed in different worlds, but shared a deep hole together. It was not only dark in there; it had a brightness you could even live in. I saw I could become Holden Caulfield. I could become Sgt. Croft. God knows what John saw he could become. But the isolation—the loneliness! All around were walls, walls, walls. Sitting there together in 1954, John and I learned, I think, not where we were, but where we didn't want to be. Bobby Plump hit his shot, but I've always thought that John and I knew we didn't entirely lose the game.

2

# Pig's Night Out

"Since you're going to Petoskey, take Hemingway's Michigan woods stories with you," Miss Wade said, her large left arm wafting toward the north exit of the hallway.

"Who's he?" I asked. "when he's not heming his way home?"

"To no point," she said. "Always to no point."

I pointed toward the library. "That way?"

"And sign your name legibly, please," she said.

"Phil L-e-g-i-b-l-y," I said, moving swiftly beyond the finger-thumper aimed at my forehead.

Each August, for six years, our family nursed an undented Plymouth four hundred miles up a two-lane highway from Muncie to Petoskey, Michigan, where on Lake Douglas a small cabin became our escape from hay fever and the threat of polio. Tom and I may have missed two weeks of daily basketball practice and hanging out at Tuhey Pool, but we got instead a lake full of bass and pike and endless acreage of birch trees and rolling hills. We saw deer and raccoons, but we knew bears were just around a corner. Someone had seen a wildcat. We stomped at snakes; we fled hornets attacking from rotted logs. On the beach, Tom, Joe Beckner, and I raced each other, built sand stockades, and invented a game—a mixture of baseball, football, and swimming. Third base was the minnow box at the end of the pier; a home run was over a line full of the Caldwell sisters' bras and sweaters we called the end zone. Joe spent a lot of time in the end zone.

At sixteen, I had become, much to my embarrassment, Miss Wade's prized student. "Think of it," she would say. "A basketball player who writes poetry." That wasn't true—I still thought poetry was for sissies, but Jack London and Ring Lardner, now that was another matter. "Never mind," Miss Wade would say.

"Either way, you've got to understand the connection between books and the world." She would tell me over and over that all great writers read each other, that writing was a collective eye looking at the world. "Learn their techniques of seeing, practice it like basketball. Look through Hemingway's eyes." It made sense. I was Bob Cousy most of the time, especially driving the foul lane and passing behind the back to a hard-slicing wing man.

"All right, Coach Wade," I said to myself, chores done and hands clean, "I'll read about Nick Adams, and then go to this Big Two-Hearted River country you want me to experience. I'll bring back a story for you." Tom was at an ROTC camp that summer, and Joe and his family had stopped coming. My mother and father shared quiet walks, the Detroit Tigers games on the radio, and hummed their own versions of Nat King Cole's "Mona Lisa." Left alone, I planned to read the Michigan woods stories first, and then make another plan. I started one sticky afternoon on the beach where Treva Caldwell was sun-bathing. I read, imagined, and began to watch through Nick's eyes as his father in "Indian Camp" turned over the Indian's body to see his throat cut from ear to ear, just as Treva turned over on her back trying to cover her breast in time. I didn't see a thing I told her by dropping my head and reading harder. By the time Nick Adams had drunkenly stumbled through "The Three-Day Blow," I was intoxicated with Treva, sneaking peaks at her slightest movement as though she might escape from my golden glass.

By the next morning, after a fantasy night, I had recovered. With permission, I packed the car with Hem's stories, my camera, notepad, fishing gear, wading boots, binoculars—everything I needed. In his "Up in Michigan" story, Hemingway writes, "Horton's Bay, the town, was only five houses on the main road between Boyne City and Charlevoix." That was south of Petoskey, and I knew that if I stayed on Route 31, I could retrace Nick's territory by noon and then, backtracking, head north of Pellston for the rest of the afternoon. By the next day, I would be across the Mackinaw City bridge, through the Hiawatha National Forest, and onto the dirt roads that ran all the way through the Upper Peninsula to Lake Superior.

But south of Petoskey was no longer "up the road" and "down the road" farming country; it had become citified, with too many signs, stores, cars, and trucks that would stalk you from behind. I wanted the Hemingway of swamp mud, grasshoppers, open fires, and the sound a fence makes when you crawl over it. I turned around, and though I know I tempted every cop on the side of the road, by nightfall I got what I wanted. Tomorrow, I would fish in the Big Two-Hearted River.

In the middle of the night, fetal in the back seat of the Plymouth on the berm of a road, dreaming of meadows and Treva and trout, I was ripped awake by godawful screams and the rocket-roar of a revved-up truck. Out the back window I could see waving arms and beer cans ricocheting off road signs and flags about Lambda Chi something. I ducked down as a spotlight sped past, spun around, and then fired into the front seat. "Anything in there?" somebody yelled. Dirt and rocks spun against the front door, and the rioters were off again. Tucked on the floorboard, I imagined them coming back, pulling me out of a busted side window, cutting off arms, tossing pieces to the wolverines, burying car parts in the undergrowth. I was afraid, but the fear was not fresh or deep. Maybe the Klepfer episode had taken me as far down into helplessness as I would go. I was even almost ready to step out and confront them *and me* if they came back.

They did—in a wild, swerving rush up to the side door. In unison six of them leaned over like swine at a trough, spaced a foot apart, and on command pissed from roof to tires, hood to trunk, as if they wanted to tear paint from metal. Not all the windows were tight. As rocks spun again against the car, I gripped the door handle, but my hand, a totally separate thing, warmly wet and sticky, leaped back and wiped itself against my pants. I didn't know, or care, what they were singing as the truck bounced back down the road like a chandelier in a dust storm.

In the morning, stiff-necked and smelling like an outhouse, I realized I had dreamed, off and on, about my hand in a grave, putrefying. My mind said, "So what! You wiped it in mud and leaves. Forget it. You're going fishing." Still, I felt queasy, as though I had gotten bruised ribs or a cut lip in practice.

I smelled the dew and felt the morning sun hot on my back. The grasshoppers were sluggish as I walked along and plopped them in a glass jar just as Nick had done. Yes, that's what I was here for. To walk in Nick Adams's shoes, to see with his eyes. I would try. I started. Story in hand, I read, "Nick leaned back against a stump and slipped out of the pack harness. Ahead of him, as far as he could see, was the pine plain. The burned country stopped off at the left with the range of hills. On ahead islands of dark pine trees rose out of the plain." I saw that too. I saw stumps and insects and two jack pines. The more I walked and read, and the more I saw that little if anything had changed from Hemingway's pages to my meadow-wet pants, I realized the lines between past and present had been broken. I was in his story; he was in my life. Fact and fiction and history were all one and this moment was real to me. It seemed that I understood why I read: I could live in a broader world; I could be more than myself.

I stopped next to a fallen elm tree and listened to the chirr, twitter, and scurry of unseen life. The burr-grass barely moved in the breeze. Looking back, I saw I had meandered in the open field, searching maybe for the end of the meadow or maybe even walking aimlessly, in no hurry, toward a trout stream. Maybe I would just sit for awhile, look back, and think of Treva. The dew was drying out and my path was disappearing. In a few more minutes that part of the trip would be gone, except in my mind.

Then I remembered I had Hem's "Big Two-Hearted River" in my hand and it was his plan I was following. He said to look ahead, listen to the sounds of the river current rushing through the cluster of trees ahead of you.

"Nick felt awkward and professionally happy with all his equipment hanging from him. The grasshopper bottle swung against his chest. In his shirt the breast pockets bulged against him with the lunch and his fly book."

I realized I was hungry, monstrously so, and foolishly had brought nothing along, not even a Snickers. I thought I had everything. What had I been thinking? Hunger was worse than a putrefying hand. I knew right then the rest of my adventure would be shortened.

I hurried toward the river, fumbling with my camera, realizing I wanted to take a few pictures. The pace of moving, thinking, seeing suddenly accelerated, and when I stopped at the bank—book in one hand, camera in the other, and the jar of grasshoppers in my armpit—I knew that Nick's entry into the water wouldn't be mine. "He stepped into the stream. It was a shock. His trousers clung tight to his legs. His shoes felt the gravel. The water was a rising cold shock." I felt nothing. I was not relaxed, happy. I was not in the Hemingway *moment*. My thinking and my body were in two different places.

I saw the other bank and kept sloshing toward it. Yet I kept wanting to stop or slow down. Something was holding me back, like an arm across my chest, and then it left me.

One more step, and I slipped on a stone. It was all over. Book, camera, and grasshoppers went flying, and I plunged to my knees. *Now,* the water was icy cold. *Now,* my skin shriveled in terror. I had no choice but to stop, adjust, gather myself. I was in the Big Two-Hearted River, all alone, and all around me the gnarled land and fractured logs were unmoved, unchanged by my disturbance.

Crawling out of the river, I knew I had not seen what Hemingway or Nick had—trout leaping into air or slipping under branches. I had not seen fine trout laid out on the grass. But cold and hungry, I had seen six guys, standing like pigs in a row. I was no longer Nick or Hem in their story, but me in mine—and I wanted a hard grip on a slaughtering knife. I knew that would pass, but it's what I saw and felt. I was sure that would be the truth I would have to tell.

So I decided right there that I would go back to Miss Wade and thank her for the opportunity to connect life and art in her way. But I'd have to tell her I couldn't see much point in practicing someone else's seeing. What I could do, though, I would say, with great affection and at some distance from her gifted finger, was try to catch my own trout in my own stream if that'd do any good. Then I'd duck.

In Muncie, the drinking age was twenty-one; in Ohio it was eighteen. We were sixteen, older in our dreams, of course, and in our swaggers and the way we talked. But we knew not to try the liquor stores in our hometown. And since MacDonald, our left tackle on the football team, was big and shaggy, we depended on his fake ID to get us into the bars across the border. We'd slip in behind him, head for a dark corner, and let him bring over the beers. After a few trips, we found a place that didn't care how old we were, a place, in fact, where we felt welcome.

Friday, the day after I got home from northern Michigan, I got a call from "Duke" Scott who said that tomorrow night at seven o'clock MacDonald, King, Mick, Whitey, Scott, and Raisor—the Purple Gang—were going to Ohio. Bring money. Tell my parents I'd be staying at his house overnight. He'd do the reverse at his place. Scotty was like that when he wanted to be the Duke. He was Scotty when he was my best friend, upbeat and open. He was Fred when he acted the accountant or committee chairman. He was Scott, the movie star. His middle name was Jewel—a punch in the mouth if you used it to his face. I'd been away. I missed the guys. I cleared the calendar for the weekend.

A road trip with the Purple Gang was always an adventure in exclusion. We wore our Bearcat letter jackets (purple and white), which relatively few students had, and we tried to make our dialogue incomprehensible to others passing by. "Hey, Mick, what's another word for *omnivorous*?" We did think of ourselves as a special group, athletes with bookish inclinations. You were usually a "jock" or "nerd" in our high school, but we would just as easily park ourselves in an Honor's Club meeting and dissect the floor play of Bob Cousy as we would turn a half-back slant into a French conjugation. We were pretentious and we knew it, but just as some students had begun to wear pegged pants, upturned collars, and slicked-back hair (we were among them), we went one step further and distinguished ourselves by outrageous wit, pranks, esoteric knowledge, and courtly manners. The simple rule was: if they can figure us out, we're not doing it right.

Scotty said that King had declared Saturday night as the Night of the Pig. We knew what that meant.

"You, Raisor," King would say. "Give us the history of the pig. And don't say 'What?' this time."

"You, Mick, stand up here. If a pig attacks you, do you jump up a tree or fart in its face? What do you mean *do both*?"

From basics, we would go to allusions, anecdotes, rhymed pig Latin—all night long we would weave the kingdom of swine into our dialogue, as we had previously done with batting averages, Hollywood starlets, battles that changed the world, and favorite dishes with beer chasers. Often as not, to honor the evening, Scotty would bring it to a climax, a previously conceived point at which a surprise guest would appear—a phone call from Dom DiMaggio, a poster of Debra Paget, a letter from Douglas MacArthur, or Hungarian goulash for six. In the midst of our finale, Whitey would stand, try to find the north ("Over here, Whitey! No, no, this way!") and stumblingly offer a toast to the ancient gods of drink (his Nordic ancestors) who had made this all possible.

Our entrance into the Arena Bar and Grill in Fort Recovery, Ohio, had become a staged appearance announced to eight or ten regulars by the single fixture at the end of the bar. We knew him as Tobin.

"They's here again. The princes of purple. Blessed we are, brothers, they's royalty. Ask 'em. Ain't no flies on theys butts."

We assumed Tobin slept on his stool and that his beer mug, never empty, was his right hand. Clouded in cigarette smoke, he still smelled like dirty socks. He had opinions on everything, so sometimes his name was Asshole or Sheer JesusChrist Idiot.

"Tobin, O Tobin," Scotty said, heading toward our round table in the corner. "Are you still screwing pigs this week?"

"Only purple ones," Tobin said. "Theys Muncie ones are sweetest."

"Hell, Tobin," Mick said. "A Muncie pig smells like you do."

"Yes," Tobin said. "We does love ourselves."

The show and the evening were on. We were the entertainers; they were the providers of 3.2 beer to the underaged. Their interest in our performance varied: we were mocked, applauded, and even challenged to take our ugly snouts outside.

I knew MacDonald had been practicing his lines since he walked in. He was our resident thespian, the one always chosen by Miss Tuhey for Oedipus and Macbeth in our class scenes.

He had a rich, low voice, and by squinching his shoulders and arching his back he could almost make us believe he was old. As we settled into our roles, with the help of a couple of beers, MacDonald went lame and hobbled over toward Tobin, dragging behind him an imaginary something on a leash.

"Mr. Tobin," he said. "This here's Clytemnestra. She wants to meet you, thinkin' you might prefer a she if you had a chance. Now, she's a Hampshire and that's to my way of thinkin' the finest breed in our two states. She's a young thing, and jus' like you, Mr. Tobin, has a small head and a trim jowl. I swear you look at her face and you think of squash. Ain't she pretty, Mr. Tobin?"

Tobin's laughter was a giggle, a huff and puff expiration of air and a wrenching attempt to prevent sound. His right hand went up in a sign of surrender.

King stepped forward, muscling MacDonald back to his beer.

"I apologize for the old fella, Mr. Tobin. He wouldn't know sow-thistle from pigweed."

Whitey was already drifting among the audience trying to find someone who would dare compare Ted Williams as a baseball player to any other stack of pancakes in the whole history of the game. Someone mentioned Babe Ruth. Another said Willie Mays could field as well as hit. Whitey told them corn syrup wasn't maple. "Hell," he said in a voice that tried to sound like MacDonald's old man. "You wouldn't know the difference between a Berkshire and a Landrace."

What is the difference? he was asked.

"Scotty?"

"I'm looking. I'm looking," said Scotty, flipping quickly through a small volume he had plucked from his pocket.

"All I know is they all die," he said finally. "And what kind of insurance policy did they have?" He walked slowly from our table into the center of the room. Someone coughed. Whitey drifted back into the dark. Tobin huffed and puffed, holding his sides from breaking loose from his body. In time, Fred J. Scott would become The Scott Group and he would garner a seat on the insurance companies' Millionaires' Round Table and the even more exclusive Top of the Table. He walked in a circle, as though under a spotlight, holding his little book close to his eyes. I knew he was conjuring up the scene in "On the Waterfront" when Terry Malloy (Marlon Brando) says "You don't understand. I coulda had class. I coulda been a contender." Scotty's jaw went awry. He got the voice as best he could, and he started, totally oblivious to the discrepancy between his Brando manner and the subject: "It says here dat da Mangalitza breed—damn that's a hard word to say—da Mang-a-litza has a small prick and a two-year life span. Now, whadda ya gonna do wid dat? Whadda ya gonna do wid dat? Give da pecker a whole term life policy? For two years? No, no. Give da little hard-on a term policy wit a hurried-up death benefit."

Tobin fell off his stool in a noisy coughing of laughter.

I wanted to keep it going, as I helped him back up, but I couldn't think of anything except a line I remembered from somewhere. "Ireland," I said, "is the old sow that eats its farrow."

I got "sow" in there, and though I didn't know what "farrow" meant, I guess it was all right, because a ditty sprung up from the corner, a jig was tapped on the bar top, a soft voice spoke from a stool:

> Oh Arranmore, Lov'd Arranmore,
> How oft I dream of thee,
> And of those days, when by thy shore,
> I wandered young and free.

The stage was now the whole bar, and I could see it would be a great evening of impromptu theater, until I felt Tobin's hand on my elbow. "Git out da back real quick," he whispered. The second sense that's natural to hunters in thick woods is natural to young lawbreakers as well. Enough said, we exited. Looking back I saw a Stetson at the swing doors in the front and a body standing like John Wayne. Tobin said, "Alcohol Control Board," but he didn't need to.

"Jesus, you stink," King said.

"Thank you," Tobin said, smiling a toothless, gumless grin that didn't disappoint us.

But we had just gotten the hook. As we headed out of town with our beers and an aborted play, we simmered. We were characters in our roles who had been banished with our lines still stuck in our craws.

"Who got too loud?" Mick asked.

"Don't be looking at me, swineface," MacDonald said. "I was in the head."

I suggested he should learn to keep his garbage in his gut, and got slapped in the nose with the empty sleeve of his letter jacket.

King told Scotty to slow down, he had to piss.

"In your pocket," Scotty said, revving the engine, and frog-jumping the car for half a block.

We let the tension absorb us like mud and then we sank into our own separate, silent injuries. When Scotty passed the city limit sign, he hit the accelerator hard, and we began to fly completely alone down the dark highway. All the windows were open, and the wind lashed us, washed us, and Whitey began to hum, then sing:

> Drink up, drink up, you'll miss the gray ship,
> You'll miss the long trip to the ale-green isle.

Slowly, we all picked up the roundelay, and then began to make up songs. No one had wanted to go into a down zone, and none of us knew why we had gone there, so even before we felt exhilaration, we quickly leaped ahead and began barking and howling,

> To do it again, to do it again
> Would shorten my life, would shorten my life,
> I'll do it again, I'll do it again,
> Bring over the bottle, bring over the bottle.

Down that highway, five, seven miles, in an open-windowed, wind-blown careening car, insanely stupid as it was, dangerous to everything that fluttered and breathed, dangerous to telephone poles and barbed-wire fences, we found the freedom fantasy we had imagined, somewhere, sometime. We didn't care that, at ninety miles an hour, we could die. We didn't even think about it. We were living. We were in the songs, with each other, wild and yelling and laughing, unfettered by parents, teachers, girlfriends. Whatever "winning" was like, it should be like this.

Give me the state championship, give me the Academy Award, give me another Budweiser, give me the energy of this pure wind, and I'll ride it like a Harley Hog without headlights.

Eventually, Scotty began to wave his hand at us, like slow down the singing, the noise. We did, and he brought the speed down. Ahead of us, we saw a blinking yellow light.

"We're here, I think," Scotty said, squinting left and right.

He came to a stop in the middle of Royerton at four o'clock in the morning. "One mile down and to the left," he said. As usual, not knowing what to expect, we lapsed into silence. Scotty's climax was at hand. He turned off the headlights as we entered an off road, the moon alone becoming our guide. The only sound was gravel under the tires. After five minutes, Scotty stopped. "There," he said. We peered through the dark, trying to penetrate the rising morning mist and the outline of a barn and further on a house. "Where?" said MacDonald. "I don't see shit." Scotty stepped out of the car, gesturing us to follow. He walked to a wooden fence, hung his letter-jacket on a post, and stepped over. We followed suit, the Duke leading the King and his entourage into a wet field and the invading smell of pigs. "Gentlemen," he said. "Your sty awaits you."

Below us, a dilapidated shed, a large pond, a mud haven, and a pen of porkers stirring at our encroachment. "Take your pick of the litter, my friends." Scotty said. "Find a favorite to talk with, share some swill, whatever your pleasure. There's more than enough for each of us. Mine is that big fat one." Gulping down his last can of beer, he yelped and spiraled down the hill as we stood stunned, outraged, and full of admiration. Scotty had done it again, taking our little verbal drama out of the abstract into the concrete. We followed his lead, drinking deep and then squawking, hooting, slopping through the dark in a wild romp among the pigs. They scattered, squealed, and as we lunged, they lunged, the mud splashing like thick syrup around us. Whitey caught a little one, tucked it close to his chest, and began walking up the hill, stroking and baby-talking as though he were carrying it to a crib. Frustrated at my own ineptness to catch anything, I sat in the mud and watched the others' peculiar dives and the contortions of the uprooted gilts.

From my position I had a perfect view of Farmer Jack and the Missus as they stormed out of the house. Amazingly, as the dawn light broke and his shotgun fired in the air, I was certain I was seeing the start of a sulky race at the county fair.

We were good at escapes. Simultaneously, we unstuck ourselves from the mud, ran low to the ground, sobered quickly, plucked our jackets from the fences, and in thirty seconds we were all diving into the front and back seats of the car as though it had all been designed. Scotty started the car, it jerked into gear, and just as we heard a siren and saw a light flashing a half mile behind us, the wheels spun and we headed out of there. We glanced back at Farmer Jack, the approaching sheriff's car, and then each other. We smiled. "My God," Scotty said. "What a hoot!" Whitey began his toast with a particularly grateful nod toward Balder and all the Norse gods from the Land of the Giants.

Then the car stopped. It stopped dead in the middle of the gravel road, and wouldn't start. We all jumped out and began pushing, and that's when Farmer Jack and a deputy walked up. I felt that that too had been designed.

The deputy addressed us as Boys, told us to stand in a straight line, pulled out the letter jackets from the car, tossed empty beer cans at our feet, took our names and, as he said maliciously, former addresses. None of us had any kind of police record, though we had had our share of skirmishes with teachers, principals, park security guards, and even some parents. But this was new territory, and we all saw ourselves inside of the Delaware County jail. Farmer Jack stood near the fence talking with his Missus, and finally, after a brief discussion with the deputy, he walked over to us.

"My name is Jonathan Eldridge. My family has lived in this county for ninety-seven years. All of our children have graduated from either Royerton or Muncie Central. I have asked the deputy to file charges against you boys. You may have destroyed our whole year's litter. *I want that to sink in.* The way you have disturbed, the way you have stressed, these pigs may cause them to stop eating, growing, or reproducing. The cost to you and your families may be considerable."

Our heads were all lowered and our eyes followed Mr. Eldridge as he walked back and forth in front of us. His face seemed to sink into a kind of pain that was neither physical nor emotional. He was trying to tell us what it was, what we had really done.

"We won't know until after February the outcome of all of this, so you boys may have to face some hard times ahead. For now, we'll let your parents know about this, and we'll see if it becomes a court matter. I don't know you boys personally, but I know you're Bearcats. I follow all the teams. You, young man, I know you, and I want to tell you something."

He was talking directly to me. I had been singled out and that meant bearing more responsibility than the others, so they pulled ever so slightly away. How had I become known to this man who I did not know? His face was rough but not unkindly, and his eyes were those of one who spent long hours watching horizons, a distant kind of look. I couldn't see where he was seeing.

"We live a hard life out here," he said. "Friday nights we clean up, my wife fixes a nice meal, and we turn on WLBC at seven o'clock. We listen to Don Burton's play-by-play. In the background we can always hear Herbie Houk's 'Yeah, Rah, Bearcats!' We listen to the game together, my wife and me, and we know the players. You're my favorite."

I didn't know how to look, where to look. Although I was being both accused and approved, I wasn't standing there for either. His mind and story were going somewhere else.

"All along, I say, if we're down by five or ten points: 'Just wait till Phil gets going; we'll be OK.' My wife nods and smiles. We know. We know. This season, at the state final against Milan, I kept saying 'When Phil gets back in, we'll be OK.' I got angry when Coach McCreary didn't put you back in. I knew then and I know now that's why we lost, and I've told everyone that!"

He was making his point to a neighbor or a table full of buddies at a cafe; then he caught himself. His shoulders slumped. "What do we do now," he asked me. "We don't have many pleasures out here, all alone, what with the kids gone and all. We love our Friday night basketball, and you've destroyed that. How do we get any pleasure out of listening now?"

I couldn't look at Mr. Eldridge, so I looked across the road toward his wife, but her eyes were on her husband and what she saw made her lips quiver. I mumbled an apology, but I knew it was pointless.

No one said a word as Scotty dropped each of us off at our houses. I was the last, and Scotty's hand on my arm as I stepped out of the car was that ineffective but meaningful gesture of support. Usually we had a hand-clasp farewell, but in the face of this reality our ritual seemed futile. We were leaving things behind, step by step, and as I walked in the back door I knew we had ended the Purple Gang's escapades in Ohio.

My mother was in the kitchen, leaning lightly on the sink. I knew she had heard. I expected that, and I expected my father to be at the kitchen table. "Where's Dad?" I asked. Occasionally, at family picnics or listening from another room to her phone conversations, I would hear my mother burst forth in an excited voice. She always seemed full of a million things to say, words and stories she had already formed in her head. Around Dad, though, she was quiet, almost maternal. He was the explosive one, and I expected him to explode when I walked through the door.

"He's down at the office," she said. "My wedding ring went down the drain this morning—it just slid off as I was washing dishes. That and the sheriff's call, he was fit to be tied."

As she turned slightly, I saw she had been crying, quietly and restrained. Then she said, "He blamed me. He's never done that before. He blamed me." The tears streamed down her face. Whatever quarreling my father and mother did, they kept from my brother and me. Occasionally, we would see a sharp look, but no follow-up of any kind. I felt helpless. "Did Dad take off the drain elbow?" I asked. "Yes," she said. "The ring's gone." I wanted to say, let me try, let me look, let me help, but she turned her back to return herself to some semblance of composure and I waited.

When she turned around, she said, "You do know you look disgusting, don't you." Brave mother, I thought, and I could almost see her mind maneuvering. Stop talking about me; talk about him. My pants were caked with mud, and God knows what my face looked like. But explanation rather than accusation was what she really wanted, and when she asked "Why?" I knew I could tell her how I felt. It was easier than talking to my father who would accuse, judge, or affirm in a matter of seconds.

I retold the story that I'm sure the sheriff had told her, but included the excruciating scene with Mr. Eldridge and his wife. I added that all the way home, in Scotty's car, in the silence of my shame and against my own wishes to deflect my responsibility, I kept thinking: "Why would they have to give up their Friday night pleasure just because of me?" It didn't make sense. What if a parishioner saw his pastor sitting in a bar; is that cause to give up the faith? What if a lawyer steals your money; is that cause to distrust the whole legal system? I tried to say I know I was wrong, should be punished, but how far did the consequences go?

I didn't want an answer then. I don't think I wanted any more than to let the questions surface because I truly felt I had hurt the Eldridges and I needed to understand why I had not thought of them. I knew now what it felt to be young and wild and foolish, but I had been taught that wildness and responsibility go together. Be different, be outrageous even, but do not violate your name. I knew I had.

My mother gestured toward me to come to her side. She was trying not to cry, trying to move beyond her own pain and take on some of mine. We looked out the window into the backyard—Dad's pine trees transported from Michigan as seedlings, my carefully clipped hedges, the alley where I spent much of my life shooting goals, and her roses. "See that one," she said. "Keep looking." She slid her arm from my shoulders and walked slowly, actually shuffled, out the back door. I don't know how much my dereliction played in her state of mind or the loss of the wedding ring or my father's anger—or the years of whatever had been her emotional life—but her exit was like hearing a wavering whistle in the distance.

She appeared in the window outside, standing in the midst of all that was familiar and safe to me. I felt relieved. She reached for a flower, looked at me as though she were only leaving for a short trip, not to worry, and then collapsed. Just like that—reached forward and then collapsed.

"Oh, my God," I shouted and knocked a chair aside as I scrambled toward and out the back door. I was used to darting left and right—the coaches said that on the floor I was not speedy, but I was quick. Usually, between one point and another, I would never think. I was at one point, then at the other. Now, I thought of her—saw her—hitting her head, and I couldn't get to the other point fast enough.

When I reached her, I started to pick her up, to carry her inside, but she held out her hand and placed a rose petal in mine. There was no wound on her head, but I swear I saw . . . "Are you all right?" I sputtered. "For God's sake, are you all right?"

"That petal's all I got," she said, trying to sit up. "I'm all right. I just tripped over that vine." Then she looked into my face as though a distant object had moved closer to her vision. "Why? What did you think?"

She waited as the fear and desperation passed, and I knew she was watching the apocalypse in my face run its course.

"I think I thought I'd lost you," I said. "I don't know. I just never had that feeling before, that you might be gone."

Her tears came back, and as she touched my forehead, she said, "You know, I didn't even think about it, but I bet you know now what Mr. Eldridge felt, what he was saying to you about losing his Friday nights." I wasn't interested in Mr. Eldridge now, but my mother held my chin softly. "Think about it. That out there wasn't about you or Bearcats, but about something they had together for a brief period every week, like a haven, that you took away. I bet you know now how they felt."

I nodded, tears starting to well up in my eyes, and anger at myself and my tears.

"Feel it all the way through, son. Don't ever do anything you won't feel all the way through. Help me up. I need to call your father."

I did, but she held me until I finished crying.

With two weeks left in the summer, I reluctantly agreed to fulfill an earlier obligation. What possessed me, I don't know, but during the spring, in a passing moment in the hallway of High Street Church, I told Reverend Pugh that, yes, I would represent our Methodist Youth Fellowship at the three-day Camp Yopemika in August. I think I was president or secretary of the MYF, so his request and my acceptance may have been pro forma. I had, once again, followed in the footsteps of my brother, a comfortable enough path, and one against which I had no particular inclination to rebel. But I was also realizing that we were not arriving at the same destinations. Tom had *won* the state basketball championship, was committed to church and community service, had a college scholarship. I kept failing or getting into trouble.

My involvement with the MYF was social rather than religious. Our family traditionally embraced Methodism, and its emphases on baptism, the Lord's Supper, and free grace. We went to church, found the staff and services comforting, and felt that John Wesley's "Twenty-five Articles" were guides not grids. I was feeling considerable guilt about our assault on the Eldridge's world, about my wildness and drinking, but not because I was offending God. I knew I was violating a prime concern of our church's founder, but I had not been taught to think in terms of original sin or penances or hellfire; I had been taught to deal with my offense against myself and others, and find a human resolution. As part of a down-to-earth religion, in my mind, I could move freely through spirit and nature without deep commitment to either. I used to say to Mick, who was Catholic, "What do you think the chances are of your God going on vacation with mine?" He'd just smile and say, "Not in the plan." I knew for Mick there was only one plan.

Camp Yopemika was on Lake Webster in northern Indiana, an easy two-hour drive from home. I just didn't want to go to this accelerated missionary-type camp. I knew we would have morning services, afternoon songfests, and evening decisions about what we wanted to do with the rest of our lives. That was a part of Methodism I preferred to leave to others.

Besides, I knew there was another reason. I had made an unwelcome discovery. Since the Klepfer episode, I had become edgy in many public situations. Once it became clear that my fight with Wayne had given me a reputation, I realized I wouldn't have to brawl my way through high school. I would, however, be challenged occasionally, and I always checked my "hole" gauge. Where was I on the scale this time? Moreover, the "hole" moved around, had disguises, leaped up in situations that had nothing to do with whose body should be jammed in what garbage bag.

I would have to give speeches at Yopemika, mingle with hundreds of people, replay the Milan/Muncie game to every new group I met. Vulnerability, failure of nerve, immaturity— whatever the adult analysis—I felt invaded, haunted, by insecurity. I wanted to go to Tuhey Pool, swim, lie in the sun.

Duty called, I guess, so I went to Yopemika. Nonetheless, if the bus we traveled in up Highway 67, full of campers from other churches in Muncie, resonated with singing, my untuned voice was absent. I was either inside my own plans for the upcoming semester or fixated on counting the Mail Pouch signs on barns. Even the anonymity of long registration and food lines, filled with excited chatter, could not draw me in. I was determined to endure, not participate, and in the end file the appropriate report.

One day into camp, comfortably alone, I sat on a log surrounded by oaks and loblolly pines. At first, I watched a mound of ants working steadily. I was fascinated by one ant carrying what looked like a piece of rice and bumping into every worker coming from the opposite direction. After ten minutes of going one way, it got turned around, at least I think it did, and headed in the opposite direction with the same diligence. But how can you tell what one ant is doing in the midst of thousands? I tried to imagine being an ant. That was like trying to be a tree. Grow. Crawl. Ants don't have an *I*, do they? I had the I, and I lost the ant somewhere in the mass.

I opened a book I had been reading—again given to me by Miss Wade who had been shocked and then amused by my Michigan woods story. "Smart ass," she'd called me, and handed me *A Portrait of the Artist as a Young Man* by James Joyce. "You want to talk about art, hunh? See if you can swallow this guy." Stephen Dedalus, the main character, was no Nick Adams. He couldn't throw a fishing line past the end of his glasses.

I didn't much like him, but I wasn't looking for any more shoes to walk in. I didn't understand him either, but then I wasn't Irish. I liked Irish but I wasn't Irish. It was years later when I read the book carefully that I realized that the line "an old sow that eats its farrow" which I had already used to good purpose was, in fact, from this book. It had gotten out of the book into general usage, or gotten into the book from general usage—I didn't know which. But I didn't even see it this time though, because I wasn't ready for Stephen's aesthetic theory. His *integritas* and *claritas* confused me. But I did get this—you walk by something time after time and never see it. It doesn't exist. Then you see it. Now it exists. Then you can get to know it, but you've got to see it, in your mind, to make it real. On the way back to my cabin I looked at plaques on trees, a marshy area, and the cedar shingles of Lookout Lodge just to make them exist.

When I crossed the old tennis courts, I saw a group of girls parading, carrying rackets as though they were batons. They filed across my path, circled me, then pushed me to the front. I was obliged to march at a steady pace, "Count in time. Count." All right, I thought, I'm with you. Imagining myself strutting on a football field, I raised my knees higher, barked evenly the cadence. I was in full control, until I heard the laughter. Looking around, I was alone. Staring and laughing at me, along the fence, maybe fifteen people had gotten the joke, fifteen who had just *seen* me. Ah, yes, now I knew what Stephen was talking about—portrait of a fool.

I was glad I had a smile on my face when I passed the young lady who had pushed me to the front. She had one on hers. I recognized her now—on the bus from Muncie. I had seen her but not seen her.

"I'm Juanita Waln, you're Phil Raisor," she said, those two names together seeming simply facts in a world she had just created. She was from Muncie, a majorette in the Central Marching Band, knew who I was, and then asked if I could tell the difference out there in the woods between a yellow morel mushroom and a death cap, as though the answer was of considerable importance. I said no, but I could distinguish between a honey bee and a killer bee and that I suspected we were talking about the same kind of difference. "Not quite," she said. "You pick the mushroom, the bee picks you." I didn't need a comeback. I was happy with our beginning.

What struck me was her ease and self-possession. Among girls as striking, I normally got the bubbly effervescence and a determined defensiveness. "Oh, the world is so electric, so alive, but no, no, I'm not dating now, not this week anyway."

The Memorial Fountain near the lake had its own symbolic meaning, but for us the next noon, it meant salvation for the thirsty and dirty. We scooped the water into our faces. After two hours in damp, open spaces and then in dense under-brush, scratching gnats from our hair and pinching leg-bur-rowing, blood-sucking ticks, Juanita and I broke from the woods. She was still laughing at my attempts to get straight in my mind the gills, pileus, stipe, velum, mycelium, the Latin names, and the clusters of color in the mushroom. A quick water-fight with our feet left her shirt pressing against her bra. She asked what it felt like in the fourth quarter of a ball game when my shirt was so heavy with sweat moss could grow.

The afternoon was different, cleaner, quieter. Her black hair may have been shoulder-length, but she had shaped it to frame her face. Although Juanita, Spanish-sounding, was only her mother's favorite name, given her soft and full facial fea-tures and her exquisite shape, it did not surprise me when her fellow campers would ask, "Habla español?" and "Do you do any professional dancing?" Her new world opened before us, and although she was the tour guide, I was the historian. Years later, I would look at "word" notes I had made about what we had seen, talked about, done: sock-hops, Waln, Scots or Welch? Wilson Jr. High, salt on ice cream, Mozambique, President Eisenhower, Ball State Teacher's College, dissecting frogs, the Globe Theatre, Milan, Madame Curie.

On this first full day together, we relaxed into friendship. Silence and watching were as much a part of our conversa-tions as were words. I found myself nodding in agreement as her eye locked on to a polished rock in the gift shop or a div-ing float slipping freely from its mooring.

By the end of the week, we had spent most of our time together at Yopemika. On the last day we agreed to meet at the fountain after the candlelight vigil in the forest. I said that no I wasn't going to become a missionary in Africa and she assured me she wasn't moving in with migrants in Union City.

About sunset I checked in with our cabin leader who said several of the campers had already headed toward the amphitheater. When it became dark, we would all meander though the forest, candles lit, and silently reflect on whether or not it was our time to decide for Christian missionary work. I knew my answer, but I enjoyed the pageantry and recognized this was an important night for many fourteen- to eighteen-year-olds.

I caught up with Frankie Thomas and a couple of guys I didn't know. At a clearing, one of them pulled out a half-pint of Jim Beam. So did the other. Frankie joined them. "Hey, pal, have a hit," the tall one said. I passed. I had taken no vows about party drinking, but this wasn't my party and these weren't my people. It didn't take me more than a moment, however, to see where this scene was going: "'No. I won't'; 'Yes, you will. What's the matter, Mr. Bearcat; we not good enough for you?'" That's the way it would go. I tried to slip past, but the tall one stretched his hand against my chest. It all seemed so out of place, almost a comedy. In the middle of a quiet woods, at sunset, during a church camp, I would be fighting over a gulp of Jim Beam. I could really pick the spots. First an ice cream social, now this.

I felt a surprising, sudden urge to smash this tall, skinny, pock-faced creep whose untied bow tie dangled down his shirt front. The emotion kept expanding: I had no doubt I could break every bone in his face. I wanted to kick him—everything I feared in Klepfer was now in me. Now I knew I had good reason to be afraid last summer.

Usually, I was a fairly reserved person, given to occasional outbursts of spontaneous behavior but never irrationally angry. Where was this coming from? I now had a temper problem to go along with my insecurity problem, and both seemed to derive from the same place. At the moment, I wasn't the least bit afraid of this volunteer for the next Crusade or a truckload of fraternity boys or even a Wayne Klepfer. The "hole" was closed. But I was one word or one gesture away from outrage. I had enough problems back in Muncie, waiting for Mr. Eldridge's decision, and I knew what scandal this scuffle could cause, but I had a rigid hand on my chest.

I saw then, he wanted to move it, but couldn't. We were, in

fact, in the old western, now classic, comic situation: who draws first? I released my gun and stepped back. I think I stepped back because of the certainty of what I would do, and my inability to control it. He thought I had chickened out. "What's a matter? You a wimp? Hey, fellas, he's a wimp!" I would have let that stand because the violent urge was quietly slipping out of me. I was feeling that I was mastering myself.

Then, he flipped me on the nose in his farewell.

I hit him in the stomach first, the head second, and shoved him into a thorn bush third. Frankie got a hard stare. The third fellow was gone.

Now, leaning against a tree, I did find the scene funny. The "punch line" had surprised even me. More than anything, I realized I hadn't felt a thing as my fist whipped out. Instinct, rather than murderous intent, had taken over. I could live with that. Hell, even the Three Stooges would slap back when their noses got plucked.

I couldn't find Juanita at the fountain. I didn't worry. Taking off my shoes, I walked around in the sand awhile, piling up mounds, and then flattening them with slow, swirling strokes of my foot. A relaxed, secure feeling had settled over me. I heard her muffled laughter and knew she was in the lake, watching me meander along the beach. Eventually, she called me over to the pier, her wet hair pulled back like a flamenco dancer. She said I looked like one of those broken-legged seabirds that wasn't going to make it. I assured her I was (Coach McCreary couldn't do without me) in spite of a frayed lateral cruciate I'd gotten working construction.

We sat on the pier, under full moonlight, as she dried out, and I listened to her talk about her best friends, majorette practice, and her life with parents and sister, twelve years younger than she was. She showed me their pictures in her billfold, and flipping through them, I stopped her at one. He was an angular, white-haired man standing on a rock overlooking a bay. The dignity and solemnity of the man struck me. "Who's that?" I asked. She cupped the picture to her as though it were a chalice. Her smile was evanescent. "I'll bet it's your grandfather," I offered. "Yes," she said. "The best thing in my life."

No explanation, just the best thing in my life.

I realized I didn't need to know why. We would spend time together, lots of time, and who Juanita was, her sound, motion, character, would come to me at her own pace, in her own way. I sat back and looked at her, deeply, to be sure I saw her.

Amazing, I thought. I hadn't wanted to come to this camp, this beach, this sacramental light, but happily, almost laughing, and completely surprised, I felt I was sitting in thick syrupy mud, free, slightly intoxicated, watching the start of a sulky race.

3

# The Titanic Clash

A few times before the next basketball season started, as I expected, I returned to the Milan/Muncie game. But no matter how hard I tried, I could not imagine myself as the hero. What would I have done if I had been sent back in to replace Aguillana? Tighter defense on Ray Craft? I would see my knees locked on Ray's, pushing him back past the foul line. Or I would drive down the middle instead of taking a set shot. But by the third picture, things would fall apart. Plump would shoot instead of Craft or I would bounce the ball off my ankle at the foul circle. My mind was determined to make me deal with the facts. The newspaper facts were that I scored no points and had two quick fouls. My own facts were that I had not played defense or made good shooting decisions. John Casterlow had solid reasons for being distracted. I had only solid reasons for being focused. At times, I blamed other players and also the coach for his game plan. Before long, though, I simply wearied of the exercise. A new season was coming. Let me imagine the future. Let me hit the jump shot at the state final this time.

In the opening scenes of *Hoosiers,* Indiana's flat land, mottled by fall colors, stretches for miles. Two-lane highways, a few trees, and scores of barns dot the landscape. At this crossroads of America, farm boys ease the cows home, and after chores, shoot at netted hoops until the sun goes down. Out of this quiet and decent life comes a state basketball champion. It is a true picture. I wouldn't have it changed. But it is not the full picture. Whether in urban Muncie or metropolitan Indianapolis, long past sunset, in the glare of headlights or hand-held spotlights, loud, foul-mouthed boys ram their bodies against each other under rusting backboards on gravel courts. Champions also rise out of these dangerous "playgrounds" where lives are just one wrong word away from a stray elbow or a knife.

"You're easy, man."

"Try me."

"I'll be round you so fast your nose'll be up your ass."

"Not if I be standin' on your face, sucka."

In 1954-55, the big-city boys dominated the regular and postseason tournaments. With all of its starters graduated, Milan bowed out early in the polls. Large schools Hammond and New Albany were picked to win their districts. But Muncie Central was an almost unanimous selection by coaches and sportswriters to win the state championship. The logic was simple: Muncie was a veteran team, which would learn from its mistakes against Milan. Yet, Oscar Robertson was becoming the best basketball player in the state, and his Indianapolis Crispus Attucks team, seeded highly in their district, might have a real chance, some thought, of beating the Bearcats. Early in the season, with both teams unbeaten, a Muncie vs. Crispus Attucks showdown was widely predicted. Said one columnist: "These two should decide the Indianapolis semifinalist victor and the winner of the titanic clash should go on to win the state championship." The opening polls had Muncie ranked number one, Attucks number two.

Indianapolis Attucks was an all-black school established in 1927, during a period of great influx of blacks from the South, white resistance to integrated high schools, and the surging political power of the Ku Klux Klan. As in Gary and Evansville, blacks were becoming essential parts of a community's work-force, but to avoid intrusion into white housing and schools they were cordoned off into their own neighborhoods. In his book *'But They Can't Beat Us': Oscar Robertson and the Crispus Attucks Tigers,* Randy Roberts observes:

> Crispus Attucks was built in the heart of Frog Island, on West Street between Eleventh and Twelfth Streets, with the foul-smelling Central Canal close to its front doors and Fall Creek flowing lugubriously a few blocks away. . . . The school was constructed to serve 1,000 students; more than 1,350 students enrolled at Crispus Attucks the first year, and the numbers increased in later years. But the school board expressed no

concern. It had built a school for black high school students, which meant that all other high schools in the city were reserved for whites.

Throughout the thirties and forties, the black community struggled to turn this symbol of segregation into an emblem of pride. It became a social and intellectual center where migrants from rural Alabama, Mississippi, Arkansas, would find an established cultural core, and music and art could flourish. Athletics, too, was one of its vehicles. In the 1940s, head coach Ray Crowe brought to Attucks an aggressive and disciplined approach to organized sports. By the 1950s, by the time of Oscar Robertson, the basketball team had appeared in the Final Four tournament and established itself as a premier program. No one doubted the quality of the players, coaching, or fan support.

In 1955 I was more conscious of race relations. John Casterlow had helped me see the destructiveness of racial division. As we traveled during the season I kept my eyes open. I found out that we could only stay in certain hotels or eat at certain restaurants when we went to South Bend or Marion because we had black players. I didn't see the overt *Colored Only* signs that I would later see in Louisiana, but perhaps I didn't walk down the right streets or stop at the right depots. In Muncie, I noticed that no blacks ate at the Elk's Club, where the Purple Gang had lunch. Why would John never join us? I noticed something else. John and I had been deeper in our understanding of each other than I had been with most of my friends. We could laugh and sit together on the high school steps or the bleachers after practice and just talk. But neither of us pushed beyond that. Our feelings could touch, but our social contact was limited. We both saw, but didn't broach, that dark territory.

At the first practice, Coach McCreary set the goals for the team. As he told *Muncie Star* columnist Bob Barnett, "We are going to play our games one at a time and try to win every one of them—right down to the final game of the state tournament. We are shooting for the big prize and don't care who knows it." Thrusting out the Muncie chest again, Coach set the expectations, and the tone, in public stone. We taunted and bragged because winning every game and the state finals seemed as real as the words. I was a believer. I was also falling for Juanita, nursing a bad left knee, troubled by my mother's failing health, worried about pigs, courts, jails, and public humiliation, and determined to get the grades for an academic scholarship (if an athletic one wasn't offered). During the summer an Air Force Academy recruiter had stopped by and said if I did well in calculus and advanced trigonometry, and had a great season, he'd be back. I began to feel new kinds of pressures. What was advanced trigonometry?

A few days after returning from Yopemika, I called Juanita. She was crying and angry, first at the injustice of life, then at her parents for breaking up their marriage for the second time, and then at me for calling. She and her mother were in the midst of packing, and why didn't I mind my own business. I said I would be over to help, if she would tell me where she lived.

When I drove up to a small, neat house on Twenty-fourth Street in southside Muncie, a mile from Ball Brothers factory, she had two hatboxes in her hands. She set them down and walked toward me. A headband held her hair tight and, without makeup, she wasn't beautiful—in the sense I had seen and been with her at camp. She was shorter than I remembered, and the blend of image and perfume I had carried with me for days disappeared. But as she stood in front of me, full of anger, self-control, and need, I saw what I would not see again for years—an unbreakable spirit that said, "Either help me say yes, or leave me alone." I touched her face. Her eyes, which didn't soften or start to cry, told me she was glad I was staying.

During the next eight months, Juanita, her sister, and mother would move five times from apartment to apartment, each one less attractive than the last. When I first met her mother on the porch of that neat little house, she was polite, distracted, and had the distinctive habit of touching her hair. I thought for a moment of Blanche Du Bois in *A Streetcar Named Desire,* a play Miss Wade had seen in New York and went on and on about. But I didn't see any vulnerability. She kept packing, talking, and the first thing she said was "Hand me that, will you?" pointing to a lamp she then carried back into the house.

Juanita's sister, Carolyn, was three. For the hour we loaded furniture into a truck, she sat in a chair and rocked, obediently and quietly rocked. She asked for nothing. I kept placing tables here, boxes there, and didn't I see that lamp earlier? Finishing up by loading some silverware and albums in my trunk, mother with Carolyn drove my car to their new residence; Juanita and I followed in the truck. We were four separate people in four separate worlds.

When my father said in December, "We won't have Christmas this year," he confirmed what we all realized: my mother was having a breakdown. Normally stylish in her dress, she would sit in her housecoat and stare out the bedroom window. I would watch her pick up a book, start to read, and let it fall to her lap. A persistent gardener, who would take personally the intrusion of grub worms into her peonies, she would start out the back door with claws and pincers in her bucket, then turn back. Hours later, the bucket would still stand on the kitchen table. My father would say every day that she was getting better, would be cooking soon, but almost every night we would drive to a cafeteria near Marhoffer's meat-packing plant. She would smile slightly if they had banana pie on special.

Catherine Raisor, Kay to her friends, was my friend as well as my mother. A tea person and a story-teller, she would hold a cup in her fingers and use it to punctuate a punch line or dismiss a foolish act. Ossian, Indiana, where she was born, "is a small town," she would say, "the size of a tack." Then she would pluck a thumbtack from a plastic case and press it into a cushion. "That size," she would say. Demonstration, concrete details, reinforcement, often witty, followed her abstractions like a snapped rubber band. She attributed this habit to two things: she had a childlike imagination in an adult body, and she was an English major. "I wanted to be a teacher or, heaven forbid, an administrator," she said, and then would smile. "But, really, I went to college to find a husband. I wanted to be a housewife more than anything else."

Her house was her business. She ran it efficiently. Files of recipes, thank-you cards, volunteer schedules, calendars, address and phone numbers, Christmas boxes, and everything else that didn't move were neatly arranged, carefully labeled. My father's job was to pay the bills; hers was to take care of him and their two sons. The lines and responsibilities in the family were clear and carefully drawn. We did not leave the yard as young boys unless we told her, but we could go freely once we had done that. Later, she was secretary of a local Women's Society, a member of the hospital auxiliary board, the church's Communion Board, and a regional philanthropic society. One year she was elected the national vice-president of the $A\phi\pi$ sorority.

I once said to her in the 1960s that if she had used those management and people skills in today's corporate America, she would have been a CEO. She shook her head. "I am of my time, and happy," she said. But then pointing to the TV and a women's march on Washington, she added, "Today, starting again, I probably would've been there."

I've wondered. Maybe my mother was a woman caught between two worlds. What would that have been like? I can only imagine that on some evenings, with her family around her, or at least scattered among places she knew, she would be in total harmony with the falling sunset mixed with the regular chimes from the Methodist church. I can also imagine her efficiently arranging with a secretary a series of conferences on women's rights to be held following her own talk to the Ball State faculty about the work of her peers in the Muncie factories during World War II. Maybe she, too, imagined herself on a bridge, looking two ways, until unsettled, dizzy with not knowing how to have both, she slipped away, temporarily, in the only way she could.

My father was very much of his time. A man's man, from a farmer and factory-worker family, he was the first to go to college. Not a man who, overtly, needed to be understood, Floyd Raisor made few claims on others and had no difficulty saying "No, I won't buy you a car, walk," and "Make your own money, boys. I make ours." We understood what he meant; "ours" was the family's sustenance, his priority, his domain. He lived without debt, expanding a porch or room, taking a vacation, only within our means. He was a high school teacher and later the director of health and physical education in the Muncie city schools. Clearly respected as a Central High School athlete, coach, educator, and supervisor, he would dispense advice and tales to young faculty and students in his office at Central High.

His advice to my brother and me could be accompanied by a razor strap on our butts and soap in our mouths. He never yelled, but he could bark in single syllables and stare down a cougar, especially if we asked for money. We did not doubt, though, that he gave us all he could. He was quick to smile, quick to support us, and though I don't remember his arm around my shoulder, I recall the look of pride in his eyes.

My father had one chink in his armor, his wife. During her illnesses, he was solicitous and quiet. He cleaned house and talked with my mother at length. I understood the depth of his feelings when, still in high school, I mentioned I knew about his anger when the wedding ring fell in the sink. He looked surprised and defensive, knowing that I had only gotten my mother's version. He patiently gave me his—but it was a broad and complicated story. I knew little about the Depression—deprivation, lost jobs, plans aborted for a lifetime, fear of organizations larger than the family, total self-reliance, suspicion of others. I didn't know that my father, six hours from completing a doctoral degree in education, had been forced to leave college to support his parents and three younger siblings. I didn't know how to sell an apple.

"Yes," my father said, "If your mother told you I blamed her for the ring, I did. She knew what was coming as it was going down the drain. Deep in me is the rage against anything lost that I have worked hard for. So easily, things can go so easily, so quickly, that you've worked hard for. But she knew also what would come next. My apology, my deep apology. Take from me my defenses against this world and I'm dead. Take your mother from me and, son, I'm nothing. At moments, I grip both like a cliff."

We entered the new year with my mother feeling better. She told my father she was in the process of saving herself. We started attending a few games, and my mother laid out a plan to attack the squirrels stealing bird seed in the backyard.

The Bearcats won the first ten games, then twelve, then fourteen.

Most athletes learn early that confidence is necessary; over-confidence is dangerous. Coaches walk tight wires trying to hold a balance. We talk of self-motivation, but most young players need pushing. Coach McCreary had one technique, packaged into four parts: shout, cajole, intimidate, plead. "My God, Raisor, can't you once run the pattern right? Into the center first, not the forward! What, you want Scott to replace you? Please, Phil, for God's sakes, think!" I would think, try again. "Now you got it!" he'd shout. We would be pleased and relieved—for a moment, then back he would come. "Awwooooh, man, what kind of pass was that?" A rhetorical question, always. "So, you've won the first seventeen games," he said, after we did. "You think you guys are pretty good. You think the media guys got it right—the best ever, hunh? Attucks is sixteen and zero. How good are they? They got their media guys too, you know." Big John had a behind-the-coach's-back gesture: open palms, wide open eyes—lifted at the same time. If Coach wasn't looking, we would all do it together.

In early February my father told me the sheriff had called. Mr. Eldridge had dropped the charges. He said no sustained damage had appeared in the pigs and he did not want to pro-long the tension. I knew the Eldridges could still have prose-cuted us for just invading their property. They were farmers. They had a livelihood to protect. I had grown up enough to know that they were part of a community that was watching what would be done. But the sheriff said Mr. Eldridge had wished me well in the rest of the season. I felt grateful for both of his responses, and wondered if he and his wife were now able to listen to the games on Friday nights. I hoped so, but expected them to find a different favorite.

When I got the news, I realized, in all honesty, that lately I had assured myself that all would work out well. King called to say we ought to try the Fort Recovery thing again next summer. Maybe this attitude was connected with our winning; maybe we were feeling invulnerable, as though Fate had smiled on us this year.

But later in February, inconstant Fate must have realigned the spheres or decided to play its own game. Other theories followed: too much pressure, breakdown of fundamentals, home court advantage. Everyone tried to explain the fact that, in the same week, both Muncie Central and Indianapolis Attucks stepped on mines, suffered heavy casualties, were ambushed and forced to retreat. We lost to Kokomo 65-63; Attucks lost to Connersville 58-57.

But in Indianapolis and Muncie, the psychological repairs began immediately. Bob Barnett, in his column, recorded the immediate aftermath of the loss to Kokomo:

> The coach [McCreary] strode into the quiet dressing room, closed the door, and looked around. Then he walked over to a blond lad slumped on the long bench. "I know what you're thinking, Scott," the coach said, "and it isn't true. You didn't lose the ball game. You fouled a couple of guys and one of them hit a pair. So what? Anybody might foul in a spot like that. We had to gamble. I sent you in to help on the press and you did it. We got the ball and scored and you helped on the play. Get that chin up. You're all right."

The point was that individuals don't lose games. The team does. The Team. How many times had I heard that? How deep did it go into my thinking? Isn't that what Yopemika was about—join the Christian team? How many times had I heard Coach draw on the military: "Act as one unit. How you going to roll over anybody if you're not a tank!" Join the army team. I realized I was being taught to think in a certain way. My responsibility was to the group. My rewards came from the group. It was the Kokomo group this year and the Milan group last year that had beaten us. I understood. I was all right with that. Then I would remember Bobby Plump's single act—a fake left, fake right squiggly, off-centered, ugly jump shot in all of our faces.

We kept hearing about Oscar Robertson. John had him pegged as an uppity jikes who needed a face smashing somewhere near the foul line. The rest of the state called him a disciplined team leader with the skills of the great ones. He was 6' 4" and both agile and powerful. He had learned the game from his brother, Bailey, who had challenged and protected him first, then left him to grow up on the courts of the black community. He got pointers from star Attucks players Hallie Bryant and Willie Gardner, but his court sense and shooting ability were simply gifts. 1955 was Oscar's coming-of-age. We read the press clippings, followed the scores. He was dropping in over twenty points consistently and was almost always the leading rebounder and assist leader. His statistics improved as Attucks' season progressed. Indianapolis sportswriter Jimmy Angelopolous, who the year before had picked the Bearcats to win the state title, picked Attucks this year. Robertson, he said, was the difference. Finally, John conceded that Oscar was a smart and savvy weapon, but he held to his face-smashing theory.

Both Central and Attucks won their respective conferences, as expected, and began the "second" season, the tournaments, in a unique way. Usually, the whole focus of the post-season play was on the state tourney, but because the two favored teams would *probably* meet at Butler Field House a week prior to the finals, the "hype" was accelerated. Even during the sectional tourneys, while Muncie was scoring heavily against Burris and Yorktown, and Attucks was winning by wide margins over Manual and Broad Ripple, the press was more concerned with the inevitable meeting of the two Goliaths. "Dream Game Looms Near" bellowed the headlines on the *Muncie Star* sports page. Indianapolis TV reporter Tom Carnegie was sure the Bearcats' knees must have been knocking together after seeing what Attucks could do to a team, beating Shortridge 93-62. The head games continued as even the Kokomo paper got into the act: "The Bearcats look tired . . . A lot of experts are on the Attucks bandwagon now. They feel that Attucks will run the Bearcats right off the floor."

In the run for the state championship the year before, I had floated like driftwood, a new piece of driftwood just fallen into the water. I was constantly amazed at the size of the waves, at the dangerous shifting currents. In this second run I was on a boat, enjoying myself, watching pieces of driftwood floating by. I wasn't the captain, but, like my teammates, one of the hands. The hazing and special privileges for upperclassmen had given way to a democracy among us. We had no "stars." Coaches, media, and the community treated us on the team as indispensable to each other. I was having two seasons of almost constantly winning, and being a major part of achieving our results. The impact on my emotions was definite: my insecurities disappeared. I gave a radio interview, spoke at a pep rally. Maybe the praying/warring image didn't hold me to the team, but linking my feelings with the community did. It reduced my fears, expanded my sense of my own strength.

The only trouble was I didn't live in a glass house where self-esteem and community bonding reigned. I lived a short distance from a telephone and a few miles from Juanita's ever-changing, turbulent world.

During the season, we would often leave our mutual "practices"—majorette and basketball—about the same time in the evening. I would be fresh from a shower; she would still be sweating in her heavy satin uniform, conditions normally fostering opposite moods. But we almost always found that as we walked toward her current residence, we entered a mood somewhere between extremes. Our hands touched, curled around our waists, and pulled our bodies toward a pale and lucid place, as calm as a small water basin. We would stay there as long as we could. People passing didn't matter. The path could be a downtown street or the rocky bulkhead along White River. That space became our cave. We could take whatever great excitement was in us or whatever fear or injustice tracked us down and make a blanket of it, lay it flat like two campers at a bonfire. If we missed out on either jubilation or despair when together, there was enough room in our worlds to pound the walls of joy or pain when we were alone. Side by side or in each other's arms, we blessed the quiet, dim light.

It was hard, though. Perhaps we were driven to our retreat by the normally unquiet and public nature of our lives. We were both performers in front of large audiences. We practiced not to make mistakes. When we did, we endured the finger-pointing and more. Yet, we must have desperately wanted the stage. We fought off all adversaries, even friends, to stay on it. To make sure we were getting better, we would even nudge each other with lovingly critical jibes. The result? "What are you now," I'd ask, "an assistant coach?" "No," she'd say, "but I know as much about a two/three defense as you know about a twirler's routine." Occasionally the critiques were sharper, and each one was connected to another move to another address. "I don't know again," Juanita would say, "but after supper last night she said this place wouldn't do. We'd be moving next Saturday." I would say I would help. She would tell me to can it.

The U-Haul trucks we rented kept getting smaller. Somewhere along the way a lamp here, a table there, must have been broken and dumped. From a first-floor apartment in a large house on Madison Avenue to a narrow one in a duplex on Mulberry, the exchanges were check-off marks on the winter map. The moves were always on Saturdays (Sunday was church day) and the weather didn't matter. Juanita's mother never gave a reason for any change of address, but money, Juanita figured, was the obvious cause. Small help came from Juanita's father.

Over the years Juanita has forgotten more and more about this period when her life was constantly disrupted and her sense of humiliation deepened. At one point, she had to live with a friend for two months (while her mother lived with a church friend) because there was nowhere else to go. At another time, she was pulled out of school and moved to Cincinnati to live with relatives; her mother thought opportunities might be better there. But each move had a common signature: decline in fortunes did not mean decline in self-image. Juanita entered each new space, and no matter the condition, cleaned it up, made it hers. While her mother worked, or tried to find work, Juanita wrote her name on the place and said she owned it. She was a mature adult at fifteen.

Only a few close friends knew where she lived. Juanita separated the private world from the public one. Vivacious at school, she was a member of clubs and choruses, and in the spring was elected a queen of the Field Day. At the after-game celebrations at the YMCA dance floor, she swirled and dipped, and then with the school dance king Pete Pippen simply cleared the field as everyone backed up to watch their performance. I would lean against the wall, still resonating with my own sense of victory an hour earlier, and watch the watchers. Their faces said, "God, I wish I could do that!" I didn't need to. I knew where she was, and I was already there.

One Sunday, I saw where her deepest strength came from. Her grandparents arrived in Muncie from Indianapolis around noon, and I had been instructed to change from pegged pants to decent slacks and a shirt that wasn't rolled up to my armpits.

"You're Phil," Juanita's grandmother said. "I've even seen your picture in the Indianapolis newspapers. Give me a hug." I stepped into her broad arms, wondering if Juanita would end up as her thin mother or her heavy grandmother. Her grandfather, the ethereal man in the picture, stood behind and laughingly shook my hand and wouldn't let me out of the hug.

Juanita pecked at her grandmother's cheek and then dove into her grandfather's arms. "My little one," he said, and they sat down on the porch swing to chatter.

I saw that afternoon what I had not seen before in Juanita— a childlike splendor. Her grandfather was a bagful of tricks, spinning spiders up a spout, constructing imaginary labyrinths, picking pennies from her hair. She laughed, even giggled, at his jokes about the red chicken with the green claws. I had never heard her ask many questions before; she was more of an opinion-giver than an inquiring mind. But now she wanted to know about the old farmhouse at Mt. Summit, Aunt Deedee's four dogs, and what it felt like to preach in a tent. When her grandfather said he was sorry about the trials they were having and he so wished he could help, she cried quietly, soft tears she had hidden or restrained. I saw her transported out of a wall she had built into the inner sanctum of his love and protection.

It was clear, I thought, that someday, when she felt less abandoned by the God of the universe, she might welcome His saving grace, but for now she had the promise that when her grandfather could really help, he would. No deity has ever had a more confirmed believer than Juanita, who smiled, and asked when he would take her home.

From the moment I stepped off the bus, again, at Butler Field House, I felt I was destined to take the last-second shot. I had played it in my mind so many times. The pass would come from Jimmy off Big John's pick. Gene would cut along the baseline, yelling for the ball. Hinds would shoot out to the side, drawing his defense with him. I would slip to the foul line, get the easy bounce, drop it in. No picture formed after that— no crowds, kisses, newspapers—just the shot. The alternative, which I had dreamed at other times, was a long, rifled pass right past Oscar's nose into John's hands soaring toward the basket. In bad dreams, sick-to-the-stomach ones, I had to keep pushing back a shaggy, nightmare intrusion of my number 43 crashing pell-mell into bleachers chased by an elusive—something.

Nothing was certain, except the walk down the dark hall toward the familiar dressing room. Instead of Wayne Klepfer this time, I saw a student manager rushing past us toward someone's voice: "We need towels over here." Around me, my teammates, loosely scattered, shuffling at different paces, silently carried their bags. All of the phrases about "commitment," "historic opportunity," "once-in-lifetime," had settled in, as they were supposed to, and we all felt the weight of our responsibility.

The weekend of March 19 was here, the semifinal tournament in Indianapolis. Assuming that both Muncie and Attucks won in the first round, the long-awaited *Dream Game,* this year's Mecca, would host the faithful. Dismissing any team at this stage of the tournament was dangerous—another Milan or unranked team could send pollsters and bookies into hiding, but the air of inevitability had blown so long that the media and fans, except those from Rushville and Columbus, clamored to get the afternoon games over with. It didn't take long. The Bearcats won by seventeen points; the Tigers by eighteen.

The form and rules of basketball, or any game, are fixed. Players and fans grow up with them. They become second nature, like a golf swing or the arm movement of a violinist. But the variables are the gym, the lighting, size of the building, playing floor, pregame warm-ups, coach's demeanor, team chemistry, and a player's state of mind. What has happened in a city, on a team, in individual lives, not known to opponents or fans, marks the game like tattoos. On another day, the death of a mother, a wrenched knee, an attack of influenza, a fight with a girlfriend might have no impact. But, then again, maybe this: "So what's she doing with that guy, what's she thinking? He's a twerp. Move your butt over, Merriweather, this is my spot. If I don't get more shots this game. I can take this creep. What's the ref doing. Let's get this ball up. God, that thumb hurts. If she thinks I'll take that crap . . ." Every coach wants a player clean, washed out, focused only on the game. That's like trying to take a day off the monthly calendar.

At the center circle, John had an odd stance. He leaned back and kept looking at Oscar's face.

I remember the game this way. It started with relief. The sportswriter who applied the Titan image to this mythic contest (Bearcats got the role of Cronos; Tigers got the Zeus part) finally left us to our own images. What I saw was that Attucks' guard, Bill Hampton, was wiry and muscular. Oscar was thinner than I expected. We all leaned into each other, shook hands, bumped, and jostled for position.

The tip-off went to Jimmy and he slipped by Bill Scott for two. Hampton caught me in a pick, slid down the line, but was blocked by Flowers. And then . . . and then . . . I lost the sense of who was doing what. Commentaries in the newspapers the next day never fit my sense of the game. "After Barnes opened the first quarter with a field goal, Attucks then hit four of its next five shots, before Hinds drove to the corner for a long, leaping jumper."

No, I stopped seeing sequentially; I think we all do. The scoreboard keeps ticking, and we know each second leads to the end of a period, but we don't play in clock time. We play in what we see and feel. A hand reaches for the ball we're dribbling, an elbow smashes against my left ear. That's Flowers free on the left, my arm's tied up, Jimmy's down, "I gotcha, Coach," Hinds signaling a two-three zone, wet spot at the foul circle, back, back, get back faster, John's eyes—lob pass, stupid shot, Phil, Jesus! up by three, slow it down, run the pick-and-roll.

At foul shots, time-outs, and halftime we look around. Preplanned, I knew exactly where my parents, brother, and Juanita were in the stands. We all tried to make eye contact. The Central band music was Souza; Attucks' combo, though, was riffing. I saw a blue-hatted man hawking red Coke cups, a box held up like a serving tray. There were more green and yellow ribbons, jackets, hats, and black faces than white faces and purple and white colors. TV cameras, tangled in cords and feet, were parked at each end of the floor. My radio guy from the Milan game was as thin as ever. I spit out more water than I swallowed. Jimmy walks around a lot. I'll bet Hampton's one tough son-of-bitch in a street fight.

This was no Milan vs. Muncie game. No slow-down, coach-crafted, mind-numbing affair; there were no posts-in-the-holes, barbed-wire fences, nor tedious flat, country land. This was a car horn, screaming tires, chicken run through downtown with the cops taking a coffee break. Of equal size and strength, Attucks and the Bearcats stuck to a strategy of fire, rebound, run. Flowers, our best defensive man, stuck to Robertson like light on a wall. Early on, Oscar missed shots and got blocked along the baseline. But Gene picked up two fouls, then three. On the other side, Merriweather was hacking his way toward a spot on the bench. At halftime I left the floor thinking how good I felt about being in this rollicking, spirited moment. Besides, we were ahead 43-40.

After I'd missed a shot in the second quarter, I'd had a sudden image of Milan, a head on a stump, a hole in it. My head. I don't know what others brought, but that was my trash for today. I missed another. Then I clipped Hampton from behind, picked him clean, and raced for an easy lay-up. No one in the locker room mentioned the two bombs. The steal, they shouted, was a fish tail flapping good-bye with the bait, and we all continued the butt-slapping, towel-waving rooting out of any debris in our minds. When we settled, Coach graphed a few plays, but mainly we glanced around, our eyes catching each other's briefly, followed by the quick nod of affirmation.

I was getting to like the tunnel we plunged into for the second half. I ran by my brother, his fist clenched, and Juanita blowing kisses. Her fingers touched mine as I passed. At the water fountain I stopped for a quick drink, and felt a light squeeze of my arm, and an unthreatening voice in my ear. "Get them niggers, Phil." I didn't see a face as the shadow slipped into the passing crowd.

I remembered an elevator, I thought of John, I was a white boy. "Good God," I thought. "Get that crap oughta here!" I realized I had seen that a large part of the crowd was black, but I hadn't *seen* it, as though it mattered. When we started the second half, the first thing I saw was that with Flowers sitting down, Jim Hinds and I were the only white players on the floor. I felt angry at my own seeing, and fought to think of a round ball and lines on a floor and striped referees and pom-poms and the score was 43 to 40. I ran up and down, guarding Hampton, inbounding the ball, but it wasn't until Jimmy's pass smacked me in the face that I began to play basketball again.

I guess that crap was in here because Indiana had its share of racism, and no all-black school had ever won a state championship. This wasn't John Casterlow and Gregory Howard Williams struggling to find an identity and place in the white world in Muncie. This was Indianapolis, Gary, South Bend, Lafayette, Muncie, Hammond, and all cities that faced an influx of black workers, ideas, and culture. One on one, no black person could survive. A group could be showered with bottles. But a whole school, intelligent, athletic, and determined, could breach a network of power that had developed since settlement. "Emerging black leaders. Watch out!" The 1960s was a blink away, and I wonder how many times during this period "Get them niggers" was said at a game or corner drugstore. And I wonder how many times young people, black and white and sick of it, nourished an unformed backlash. Coalitions are not born out of ideas, but in the guts of people learning how to think and feel.

In the second half, no one took over the game. My brother told me later that it was like watching two horses in a photographic finish down a whole stretch of track. "What did you watch then?" I asked. He said he watched the flanks, Hinds and Flowers, and they stayed too far out, but the Attucks forwards, he didn't know their names, wouldn't collapse and let them shoot the long ones. They closed out there with them, and that left room in the middle. Merriweather fouled out, and John had a field day with his short hooks and rebounding. Both Attucks guards, he said, were quicker than I was, but Jimmy was quicker than anybody. The stuttering steps of the four of us raised a lot of dust, so to say, but the pace of the game was steady. The funny thing, he said, was that the score kept going up, and so did heart pressure, hats, voices, stomping levels, and whole cheering sections, and everything was chaos in the stands, but down there on the floor no one broke off, no one seemed winded. "All of you just kept running and running like your hearts would break if it all stopped."

Tom said he had to be truthful. If he were a coach he would take the film after the game and break it into parts. He would show the one-on-one play to recruits and Kiwanis Clubs on the rubber chicken tour. At any point, he could show how to play and not play defense. He could use the example of when the score was 50-49, and Jimmy split the two Attucks guards with a nifty move down the lane. "Number 14," he said, "crossed his left leg over his right instead of staying low and shuffling. Jimmy ate him alive." He liked me getting in there and rebounding with the big guys, "shows some guts," he said, "but did you know where your man was? That was your responsibility flying down the floor to put Attucks ahead 61-59."

One clip of film he said he would show over and over was the incredible contest between Casterlow and Robertson. "Nothing like it I've ever seen. The two of them went at it. I mean it was personal. They used all the tricks. I'll bet they'd studied the films and scouting reports of each other more than anybody else. Sometimes they were so close at the rim, they looked like one body. The one Robertson hit at the end of the third quarter must have steamed John at the break. He came out in the fourth and twice went right up in Robertson's face. He brought us within three. Then there was that slump. You guys got down 67-63. That's when the Coach took you out. That's when you were finished for the day."

I was. Once again, at the end of the game, I was on the bench. This time I had committed a fourth foul, grabbing Hampton's hand as he twisted by me. I was tired. Was I also scared? Did I just need a break? Was I in the hole? I felt like I was being chased. On the playing floor, just as I saw Scotty come in for me, I had one brief moment of wondering if I was afraid of taking a last-second shot, if, in fact, I had bailed out before I might get the chance.

That's what the hole does. It wants to become the reason for everything.

I remember the last thirty seconds. Scotty had pressed aggressively, flipping loose a couple of balls. With Hinds and Casterlow hitting fouls, and Flowers tipping in a missed shot, we closed to 71-70.

In the last eleven seconds, Scotty forced Hampton to fumble the ball out of bounds. I saw the Duke grab the ball, and I knew what he was going to do. It was not in his mind, not in his nature, to call time-out. Time *could* run out. The time to win the game was *now!* How else do you play—if not straight into the risk? He waved Jimmy down the floor, yelling "to Hinds in the corner! Fire it to Hinds!"

At mid-court, Jimmy did, and the ball streaked past John's nose toward a wide-open Jim Hinds.

Randy Roberts records in his book on Oscar Robertson and the Attucks Tigers that

> All things considered, it was a fine play, except for one crucial factor; it was exactly the play Robertson expected. Throughout the game, he had observed Hinds' tendency to break for the corner; he knew it was the shot Hinds would want and the eas- iest one to set up. . . . So when Hinds broke, Robertson broke in front of him, jumping high to intercept the pass. Then he drib- bled toward the empty space and just before the final buzzer lofted the ball toward the rafters of Butler Field House.

The floor was very much a sea of black as it had been a sea of white at the end of the Milan game. All the players tried to find each other to shake hands, the usual sportsman's ritual. I got a pat from Bill Hampton and nods from a couple of others. All four of the starting guards had scored eight points each and had about an even number of assists. Oscar had dropped in 25 points, and John had 21. I reached to shake Oscar's hand, but it was extended toward John's.

"A war," Oscar said.

"I know, man," John said. "You did great."

"You, too. You, too," Oscar said.

I watched them looking at each other. Then I watched them understand. I don't know what they understood, but they were looking past the eyes into something deeper. Only a year ago, I had done that with John and seen a friend, someone who would understand without words. But Oscar and John had gone somewhere else, I thought. They weren't on the same team, but they were in the same place. I thought of Scotty and how we would share our pain. Maybe Oscar and John had no teams, only something more compelling.

I didn't know what to do with that. But I reaffirmed, as I had done with John, that I would try to break down the walls around me. I would try to see what John and Oscar saw.

When I started toward the player's room, I felt Juanita at my side, saying nothing, slightly touching my wrist with the back of her hand. Maybe I would never be back here again, maybe we would not see this together. We stopped and watched a frenzied crowd, masses of people milling on the floor, and a whole cheering section in purple and white bent over, heads down, crying as though a second time was unbearable.

Juanita simply stroked my arm, walked with me down the dark hallway. Slowly, I began to feel I was in a quiet place.

# 4

# A Cache of Silver Dollars

Our senior year. I could never understand those who thought of it as an end, a kind of drive-in theater where we all gathered for a last movie, drank a few beers, signed the yearbook, and sadly parted forever. "You were one swell fella. Sorry I didn't get to know you better. May you succeed in all you do. And always remember the night we toilet-papered Mr. Rice's front yard." For some, I know, our last year in high school was a collective farewell to a way of life we were being forced to leave. Each Saturday was "memory weekend," and even the senior prom, months ahead, was homage to our old favorite songs and the honors we'd won.

Then, there were the new James Deans bursting on the scene with family baggage weighing down their deeply troubled souls. They were alone in a universe headed for destruction or, at least, for a head-on crash with Mom and Dad. I had been through that with Holden Caulfield, and my family, unlike his, had laughingly accepted our differences in age and responsibilities. Mine were to cut the grass, pay for my gas when I used the car, be respectful, and stay-the-hell-away from Mr. Eldridge's pig farm. I felt the pull, though, of *Rebel without a Cause* and Jim Stark's need to be both tough and sensitive.

But I knew where I was going. I knew what I wanted.

My senior year started in September, untroubled and promising. I had it all planned. My planning began one afternoon as I sat in the backyard reading a piece Miss Wade had given me. Once again she had insisted I return to Ernest Hemingway. "He just won the Nobel Prize for literature," she said, "and I know he has something to say to you. He didn't get that prize by not having something to say to you." I was sure Ernest had me in mind when he wrote his Nobel Prize acceptance speech, so I said that I certainly would read what she was handing me, pleased that it was short. After the last Michigan trip, I felt removed from Hemingway. I enjoyed telling stories, and was obsessed with reading, but I wasn't interested in becoming a writer. I had enough difficulty writing letters, so I was surprised when one of his paragraphs struck me as applicable to playing basketball:

> For a true writer each book should be a new beginning where he tries again for something that is beyond attainment. He should always try for something that has never been done or that others have tried and failed. Then sometimes, with great luck, he will succeed.

That's what I could do this year; I could try something new. I could, in fact, try a style of play I hadn't seen before. Not even by Bob Cousy. What was that? I didn't know. But that's where my planning started. I would read, study, and think of how to pass, shoot, and run in a different way. I began the year excited and dreaming of glory.

The first thing I did was read my press clippings. My mother's scrapbook was a growing collection of pictures, feature stories, headlines, statistics, letters, and game-by-game summaries. My brother's scrapbooks had a sense of wholeness about them; the entire season, through his victories in the state championships, was carefully cut and pasted. Mine stopped, in the previous two years, at the pregame coverage of Milan and Attucks. The losses were not recorded. In their absence, I could feel my mother's sudden sense of disappointment, rejection. But she began again dutifully cutting up papers and magazines in September. I read that Jimmy Barnes and I were to be the stars this year, and that quickness and speed, rather than the size and power of the past two years, would be our strategy. I gathered that Coach McCreary had started talking to the press again about the time we started practices.

The summer was fading like a slow-walking old man and autumn was not yet rising to peck at his pants. Getting back in shape, I ran hot, unbroken miles in my sweat suit and new Converse low-tops. I was like a child in an open field, who should have learned safety, suspicion, who should have known by now that an attack on vulnerability was destiny's favorite weapon. But I had remained eternally optimistic, as though stupidities, miscalculations, and defeats were inherent in a system which finally prized and rewarded the diligent. I had based my self-control on being blessed in that world, always ready to overcome temporary incursions. Then, in a three-day period, I was blindsided.

My first mugging came amidst sweat and laughter.

*September 13*—I thought playing handball would help my quickness. Scotty and I met every afternoon in the school gym. My left knee was shaky and sore much of the time, but one truth I had learned: every cliché we used served the purpose of not thinking. If a knee hurts, say "Be a stand-up guy," or "Battle through it!" Acceptance of pain by cliché is as critical to success as who you know, not what you know. I would fall, crash against walls, hobble back again like a real trooper. Then, one day, with one play left in a tied game, Scotty smashed a low liner along the floor. I dove at a strange angle and got both legs under me. We heard a simultaneous double pop. Scotty says I screamed, but I remember only my thoughts: "No pain. No gain. No pain. No gain. No pain. No gain. No pain. No gain."

*September 14*—When Dr. Brown's shadowy hand turned the bright light on the screen, I asked, "How bad is it?"

"Son, now listen to me," Dr. Brown said, holding up an X ray in each hand. "The lateral cartilages in both knees are destroyed. Look here," he said, pointing with his thumbs at similar areas in each picture. "From the femur, here, to the tibia, there. That's where the fragments are, in there."

I looked past his thumbs and imagined confetti floating between ghostly bones. Those were my knees, crooked and comical and totally disconnected from the knees I was standing on, leaning into the light.

"What's it mean, Doc?" I asked, looking past him to my father sitting with his fingers pinching his lips. His broad forehead and receding hairline were bright with thin perspiration.

"I'm sorry, son," he said. Dr. Brown spoke softly, breaking from his precise enumeration to an almost dirgelike lamentation. He was a longtime Bearcat fan. "I would say that your season's over. It may even be that there's more carnage in there than I think. If so, you may never play serious basketball again."

I thought. "Boy, I'm glad that's over. Now, let me hear what Dr. Brown says." I was sure I had concocted the worst in preparation for a sentence I would hear, not like, but could live with. Maybe an operation at the end of the season, heavy casts, lots of rehabilitation.

Dr. Brown said nothing further, and I felt my father's hand on my shoulder.

"Wait a minute," I said. "Whoa, whoa, whoa. Let's wrap these knees up, make it tight, and I'll get on down to practice."

"I'm sorry, son," Dr. Brown said. "We can't do that. Thirty years from now you could be a cripple."

I slowly backed toward the door, away from this antiseptic doctor and those skeleton knees still hanging in the light. "Jim Hinds is a walking advertisement for gauze and tape," I said. "He lived with pain his whole career, and he played. This is my year, Doc, my senior year."

Dr. Brown smiled, a knowing, acknowledging smile that said he appreciated my spunk, but not my medical sense. "Jim had medial damage, Phil. But I expect both your ACL and MCL are flat out wastepaper. Your knees will lock when you're sitting; you'll collapse when you turn sharply left or right. They'll have to carry you off every game."

"Dad?" I said. I had never seen his face so unshapen. I wanted him to say, "Look, Doc. Let's let Phil decide." Or better. "I think the young man can take it. Let's let him try." But with all his knowledge of health and physical education, he probably knew what Dr. Brown was talking about. I could see that he was struggling. Finally, he shook his head, "No, son. You will not destroy your body over this."

I was amazed. Neither the doctor nor my father understood what I had to do. It seemed perfectly clear to me. We had lost Hinds, Flowers, and Big John to graduation. Jimmy Barnes and I were the leaders. We had to get to the state tourney this year. We had to get scholarships to college. And I had just picked up the national Dell magazine preseason picks for top players in every state; there I was—listed right behind Oscar

Robertson and Frank Radovich from Hammond. Now, we couldn't be talking about *not* playing basketball this year. That didn't make any sense. We needed to be talking to Coach McCreary about needles, braces, heat massage—whatever we could get in the training room.

I sat in Coach McCreary's office, a room full of championship team photographs, and began my campaign. I pointed to pictures of numerous players who had bad knees and played. I told him our whole front line this year would probably be sophomores; they would need my experience to lean on. I told him I would even sit the bench, share playing time with Scotty or Tommy Curtis. I told him . . . and then he stopped me. "We've got a new wrap," he said. "One that holds a silver dollar against the cartilage. Keeps it in place. We tape it very tight." I saw him smile as he saw me rise slowly from the chair, almost trembling, almost ready to dance. "The doc will have to agree; your father will have to agree."

All I needed was a small opening. This was it. I gathered literature on the new brace and attacked. My father was impressed. The doctor knew about it, but was skeptical. Both of them, I understood, were thinking long-term and of their responsibilities. I sympathized, walked straighter, said the knees actually felt better, promised to ice them after every practice, and agreed to quit if the brace didn't work out. I suppose they knew I was stretching that, but they saw I wouldn't give in. Finally, the doc said he would monitor my progress. Dad said he would follow the doctor's advice.

After the first practice, full of wind-sprints and leaps up the stadium steps, I knew it would be a long season. My knees stayed in place, but I was stiff, slow, and distracted. I ran in mud. I heard sucking sounds.

*September 15*—My mother remembers that I jumped up from the kitchen table and dashed upstairs when the phone rang. I remember twenty minutes later coming down to cold ham, beans, and warm milk. In between I could hear snippets of *Amos and Andy* on the radio, a dog barking in a neighbor's backyard, and Juanita telling me that she and her mother were moving again. It was 6:37 P.M., and thirty-one seconds. They were moving to Indianapolis to live with her grandparents. I don't remember saying anything. Her grandparents and mother had agreed there was no other choice, Juanita said, and she would enroll at Indianapolis Howe. She would be there at least the whole year.

"The whole year?" I asked. I watched a fly against the window, darting and dead-ended, unable to escape.

"Yes," she said. Her voice was calm and informational. She said her grandfather was able to bring them home. He'd done what he said he would. Juanita said she didn't know what to do.

Then she stopped talking, and for five minutes we sat in silence.

"Not this year," she said. "Please, not this year." Her voice was muffled and hesitant, as though she was talking away from the phone, toward her mother or grandfather, but she came back again, and her voice began to break. She said she was torn apart, loved me, had no other choice, no other place to stay in Muncie, no say in the matter, no one she knew at Howe, no friend to take with her, hated all this moving, all this endless moving.

I cranked open the window and let the fly out. I saw I had been making marks on a pad—crooked marks, jagged marks, lots of circles. Juanita said she could hide, run away, live with her father, NO! she knew he didn't want her. Good God! What was she to do? I said I didn't know, I loved her, I didn't know.

Another fly buzzed at the window. Had it come back in? Probably not. All flies looked the same. I thought of the ants I'd watched at Yopemika, and the one I wanted to distinguish from others but couldn't. Maybe we're all the same. Maybe we're locked into patterns we must follow. I guessed that would be all right if it weren't so sad, if sadness and confusion weren't so much a part of it. I asked Juanita if she wanted me to come over.

The pause was long and the "no" was soft and almost silent, almost only a breath, as though wind or tears had caught her in flight.

Hemingway hung around like a frayed and stinking sweatshirt. Now, not before, was his time for me. But I dismissed all his business about "new beginnings" as an old man's nostalgia. His Code, though, culled, without Miss Wade's direction, from his early stories and novels, became mine. "The world's going to get you, so you better get ready for it." That was perfect. I saw now in this world that victories and pleasures finally give way to resounding defeats, and self-control comes only from expecting failure. I knew now how to deal with emptiness. That view felt good and therefore was good. I didn't expect anything from this year—except more losses, more disappointments.

The losses started early.

"Cold Bearcats Dumped, 52-39"

"Bearcats Outgunned by Slicers, 85-76"

"Sharp-Eyed Bears Whip Cats, 80-66"

I became the poster-boy for the *Muncie Star:* "Raisor's knees gave out. He had to be helped from the floor the first time it happened, but was able to limp off unaided the second. Incidentally, Raisor wears a silver dollar taped to each knee for the purpose of keeping things in place, but the wagon wheels failed to do the job." The world without Hinds, Flowers, and Casterlow was a different world. Occasionally we would rally, beating Hammond and Dayton, and then fall back to defeats by Logansport and Anderson. At some point, it settled in that losing was more probable than winning. For the Muncie fans and players the expectation came first as a shock—we hadn't lost this way for a decade—and then as grumbling discontent. The communal link of the last few years was broken.

I listened to the grumbling and grumbled myself. I pushed harder, angrier, diving for balls on the floor, racing uncontrolled down the foul lane. Once, I got my three false teeth smacked back in my mouth by a low post behemoth who had the sharpest elbows I'd ever seen and felt. As he picked me up, carefully not touching my bloody face, he said quietly, "You don't belong this low, not this low." I wish I could say I went out and hit four in a row from above the foul circle, but I didn't. I just sucked the blood that kept pooling at the juncture of my teeth and gums, and went down low.

Often at night, sullenly leaving my books unopened, I gravitated toward the discontents and malingerers who hung out at the pool halls on South Walnut Street. Dirty, smoky rooms, walls postered with hot rods and stretching blondes, an occasional burst of anger, but mainly the steady clack of balls and edgy talk:

"My old man's been a pissed-off drunk for forty years."

"Shut up, you don't know squat. Wait'll he ends up like mine, dead in a back alley in Anderson."

"What for? Eight ball in the corner."

"How the hell I know what for! A nigger knife in his back's all I know."

"You, boy, what you comin' in here for?"

"Fuck you," I'd say.

"I'll rack you with a rack, you little shit."

But the griping and moaning weren't enough. With each crash to the floor, each loss, each locked knee in the classroom, each phone call to Juanita which ended in silence, I felt an expanding sense of betrayal. I sensed a conspiracy starting to slip through the halls of Central High, into the sports news rooms of the *Muncie Star,* behind my booth at Orv's Drive Inn—wherever eyes would fall on me with sympathy, but, I knew, envisaged my downfall. I expected Dr. Brown or my father to pull the plug any day. I expected Coach to say Scotty would start the next game. I expected another desperate shot clanging off the rim, another loss. I expected Juanita to tell me she was dating a Howe football player.

After practice, during the week, my knees throbbing, I would walk, keep walking, until my ankles were numb. I would walk past Juanita's old apartments, and then find my favorite drunk on Adams Street to sit with and mumble together. I would squat beside the legless man on his cart outside of the post office and listen to his train wreck story in all its variations. I tried to enter the space where their eyes and brains were, to feel, as my mother had counseled, all the way through what they felt.

I thought I saw where they were—in a world of day-in, day-out changeless futility. But I could only lie to myself for awhile. They were further than I could get. I knew I was still seeking causes or penance or miracles or conspiracies, and they were past that. They had reached below futility to hope—the hope that they would die, now, in this moment, with this breath.

By coincidence, another joke of fate, Juanita came back to Muncie for one weekend in the fall, the Friday we played an Indianapolis team—not Howe but Tech. Still, I felt the whole of that big city descend on us, and we lost by a wide margin, 63-44. Juanita didn't care about the game and tried hard to discover a niche where we could be comfortable together. But she was adjusting to Howe. It was not unlike Central, and she had made new friends in choir and cheering block. As I expected, she had been nominated for Spring Queen. Living with her grandparents, even in small quarters, was the first sense of security she had had in two, maybe three years.

I knew that what I was hearing I should hear. I wanted to hear that she was not unhappy. I wanted to hear that time was passing, and before long we would be together in Muncie. But she watched me with eyes that didn't understand my restless, abrupt ramblings, my bitter tirades she'd never heard before. I said I wouldn't be going to college. I'd probably join the army, and maybe my ROTC brother would be my goddam lieutenant. I said I would try to write her. I let her leave that weekend thinking I would see her, maybe, when she got back. I sat in my room most of the night, wondering what in the hell I was doing watching my senior year pass in silent, sullen discontent.

It was not over. Occasionally, I poured a few shots of my father's Seagrams Seven, hidden under a kitchen cabinet, into a Ball jar, and slipped out to the garage. I thought it helped me see more clearly and understand better my drunk pal. I even thought, as I walked boldly through the dark, that divine intervention had saved me and made me feel stronger. I didn't feel like a kid drinking beer, but a man facing his problems. One night, hearing myself mumble and explain something to some shadow in the night, I even sounded like my buddy. It sounded true for him, but stupid for me. I didn't want to go that far. Maybe this was another form of the hole, and I couldn't see through its camouflage. I tossed the jar in an open field.

What I didn't see, though, as I grew more isolated, was that it affected how I played the game. Scotty saw it and came down on me in a rage.

"What the hell's the matter with you?" he shouted, after another loss, after another after-game wake at his house where the Purple Gang, in better days, often gathered. "You're playing like the game's a gang fight, out of control."

"I do flop around," I said.

"No," he said. "I don't mean the knees. I mean . . ."

"He means," Bob Wilhoite said, entering the room, "that you're playing for your goddam self and not the team."

Bob Wilhoite was Scotty's stepfather, an accountant, a rigid man, whose smiles were brief and thin. He tabulated our conduct in columns. He kept time schedules for Scotty, and Lord forgive him if he arrived home past midnight with Bob's car. Dressed in khaki pants and undershirt, his favorite lounging attire, Bob would point his thick cigar in your face and say his piece. "Phil, your ass ought to be on the bench, stuck on the bench like a paperweight. You were always poker-faced out there, but now you're frozen-faced, mean, and self-absorbed. You're scoring points, but we're losing." I couldn't dispute his facts or anger. I knew he wanted his stepson to play, but tough as he was, he was perceptive and honest. Over the past five years, he'd welcomed me to his home, welcomed Scotty's friends with sometimes abrasive but often good humor. I listened to his harangue, and realized no one else was telling me what I was hearing and what I realized myself.

Scotty seemed embarrassed, but said nothing until Bob left the room, and then quietly he said, "I'm sorry about that."

I smiled. "Yeah, but you were going to tell me about the same, weren't you?"

He nodded. I sat back in Bob's favorite green chair, and looked at Fred Scott. He was a mixture of small-town farm boy with crew-cut blond hair, whose alcoholic father had abandoned the family, and street-smart tough kid who wouldn't back down from weighty tackles on the football team. We had never argued. For three years, Scotty had played third guard on the Bearcats. He was a tough defensive man, better than me, and sometimes would eat me alive in practice. Always supporting, encouraging, challenging me to be better, he had said nothing about his role, about his feelings. I had never seen bitterness in his face.

But now, through his disappointment with me, I could sense the surge of what he wanted to say, but wouldn't. "Say it," I said. "Say it, damn it!"

"All right, all right, you think I want to come at you, want to say I'm a better ball player than you, have always been, that I can shoot, pass, run better than you ever could, that you got the lucky break and I didn't, that with me in there we would have beaten Milan and Attucks, and we would have won a hell of a lot more games this year. You want me to say that, right? You want to see in me some gnawing feeling that I've had to live with. But you got it wrong, pal. I didn't resent you *or* Jimmy. You were a genuine floor leader; you could inspire the team when it was down. You could do that, and I admired the mystery of that. But this year you got blinders on and a back-of-the pack mentality. Yeah, you're damn right. This year, this fucking year, we could've won more with me in there, and that asshole McCreary can't see past the past."

We sat quietly for awhile, the wash of his words flowing over us and then away. He stood and said, reflectively and slowly now, "This year you had the opportunity but not the spirit; I had the spirit but not the chance. That's unfair, but I've learned that I was right all along. You take what you get, you dig to the bone, and the hell with the consequences. I feel good about myself, and look at you, you don't. And, Phil, I'm truly sorry for you about that."

Our regular season ended in March as it had begun in September—with low expectations for the tournaments. Although the sportswriters agreed that in the last third of the year the young Bearcat front line had stabilized and meshed with the veterans, they didn't think our record of nine wins and eleven losses promised much advance beyond the sectionals.

I had scored 20, 18, and 24 points in the last three games, which we won, and those came, not in selfish rage, but in tempered, conscious play with my teammates. Scotty and Bob Wilhoite had opened my eyes beyond what I had seen, and I adjusted to the minds and bodies around me. But I knew I was still trapped in my hole. If it had all begun with Juanita's departure and the knowledge that I would not play college ball, I knew I had sunk to an emotional tyranny that was now beyond its source. I wanted to stay with the blind passion I had felt when I almost hammered the kid at Yopemika. That sense of mayhem seemed to keep me from collapse. I could fail now, this year, no prizes, no teddy bears from the carnival, and that was all right. I could survive anything if I didn't have to hide.

The skeptics were not quite right. We won the sectional and regional tournaments and, once again, got to the semifinals, as we had the year before. In our afternoon game against Scottsburg, we were the underdog and, amazingly, had thousands of fans on our side at Butler Field House. I was not so foolish as to think the gods had turned kindly, nor had I abandoned my Hemingway code, but Scotty's formula was closer, more personal. Take what you get; dig to the bone. Against a much taller front line, we were clever, and rotated our defenses to surprisingly box them out. I was actually getting rebounds down low. When Scotty briefly replaced Jimmy in the second half, I asked him if his family owned this damn burg, would they please give it to us. In the third quarter, Scottsburg's 6' 6" center, Laverne Altemeyer, dominated us all, scoring seventeen points. We trailed the rest of the way.

As I realized in the final minute that we would not win, the rage came again. This was my last basketball game, ever. When, in the last few seconds, Scottsburg guard Jennis Stidham held the ball in the corner, as Bobby Plump of Milan had done two years before, I lunged at him, stumbling forward. Most of the crowd of fifteen thousand probably thought my knees, once again, were giving out, but the fans closest to my fall saw my eyes. They knew I had tried to ride his back to the floor. Among the mix of cheers and tears at Scottsburg's 66-59 victory, and the sympathetic gestures of teammates and cheerleaders helping me up, I heard the boos of those who had seen into my heart, and their disgust walked me off the floor.

It took my brother, though, to pull me from the depths. Now a junior at Michigan and the recently elected, incoming president of Beta Theta Pi fraternity, Tom invited me to a campus weekend jubilee. He said it would do me good to see life beyond high school. After the basketball season was over, and I began to get a month's distance from braces and bitterness, I began to think maybe the army or selling used cars wouldn't work. College was possible, if I got a full-time job somewhere or an academic scholarship, but nothing was on the horizon. Early in the season I had received numerous inquiries from basketball programs, but I guess the word about my knees got out. My father was handling any calls or letters now. I had turned away. Tom said a party would do me good, and I asked him, as soon as I arrived, where the beer was.

The impressive oak door of the stately Beta House opened to a view of a wide, curling stairway lit by an opulent chandelier. My well-mannered brother introduced me first to the house-mother, "brothers," and pledges. I met the janitor. I met the fraternity bulldog. But I stopped Tom before I got to the cat because a beautiful blonde, dressed in an off-the-shoulder green silk dress, was cascading down the stairway. Tom told me she was the girlfriend of one of the graduate students, and her eyes, that look she had, embraced everyone, not just me. After three sloe gin fizzes, I didn't believe him. I don't think she felt cornered when I pressed close to her at the bar, but she moved deftly away, as she did several more times. I wasn't being unpleasant, just persistent, feeling that I was an adult, could hold my liquor, and was as good as any graduate student.

Tom said he dumped me in bed at two in the morning, after I had created a scene. Apparently I had tried to touch her hair and drew the wrath of her boyfriend. I remember Tom called me an idiot, and he said it again the next morning when I vomited in the bathroom. After throwing me in the shower, pushing me to dress more quickly, and stuffing toast down my throat, he told me I had an appointment.

"For what?" I mumbled like my street partner in Muncie.

"You're going to meet Coach Perrigo, our basketball coach. He knows about your career, and I set up a meeting with him."

"What for?" I asked. Tom had learned the finger-thump from Miss Wade, and he connected. "Think for a moment. Just think."

"Hey, brother," I said. "I can't play basketball anymore. What is this shit?" I could feel the anger coming back, the ghosts rising, and I wanted the dead put to rest. "I'm out of here," I said.

Tom held my arm, and then jerked me to his face. "You little chump. You've been swimming in self-pity all year. Dad knows. I know. Even Uncle Om knows you got your sights on yourself instead of the rabbit. You don't even know what the operation will do. Dr. Brown says there's a 40-60 chance you can play again. That's not much, but, hell, it's something."

"You don't know what it feels like. You just don't know."

"My God, Phil," Tom shouted. "I'm not talking about what it feels like. I'm talking about your chances. I'm talking about the way to look at things. I never knew a Raisor in my whole life who quit before he was dead."

I watched him back up, as though maybe he was going to wash me out of the family, right then and there. "You make up your mind, little brother, you make up your mind now if you're going to keep up this self-destruction or get out here with the rest of us."

I threw up again, and then a second time. I coughed and hacked and coughed some more because I didn't want to stop. I didn't want to say I could go on. I didn't want to say I would give up failing. I didn't want to say I would give up the rage.

Without it, what could I do? Without it, what would happen to me?

I sat on the grass and sobbed. The last time I had cried was in my mother's arms, when she asked me to feel everything all the way through. Now I was crying again when my brother asked me to put aside my feelings and get on with my life. How do you do one or the other? I didn't know, but as I let myself go, as my brother's anger and patience waited on me, as I sank down to where I could finally see with some clarity . . . I saw I wanted both.

Slowly I got up, sensing a kind of self-definition invade me, a kind of being taking shape inside. I waited with Tom, and what he saw I'm sure was what I felt—my self-loathing slip slowly out into the cool Michigan air. I said let's go see your coach.

When I returned to Muncie, my first letter to Juanita was like a class essay—thesis, body, conclusion. It was long, serious, and full of details from the text of my life. I knew it was boring, but I poured out a year of fear and trembling, love and confusion. Her return letter was brief, humorous, and consoling. For the next few letters, I condensed, wrote and rephrased, deleted and polished. I added some notes from newspapers, a line or two of a story or poem, a piece of conversation—some of which she liked, some which she thought "pedantic-sounding." What did she want to hear in my letters? How did she want to hear what I had to say? She said to make my day come alive, not the whole day or week, just where I was at a moment, where she could see me. She wanted to hear I loved her, and that I wanted to hear her thoughts and feelings. I began to realize this letter writing was easy for us, a chat without a dial tone at the end. I began to relax into the writing, even looking forward to it.

I also looked forward to Coach Perrigo's letter. When it came, I wasn't surprised. He wouldn't be able to hold a full scholarship for me, but if the knee operation was successful, I could "walk on"—at my expense, of course—and we'd go from there. Since the Michigan trainer had examined me, I was befuddled even at this possibility.

I then read the letters in my father's file from coaches around the country. Some of the interest in me was clearly based on news clips and scouting reports from my first two years. Some was based on current information, and the coaches wished me well in my life. But one coach said, enthusiastically, that he was still in the running. He said he knew about my knees, but modern science and physical therapy were marvels to behold. Knowing what Dr. Brown had said, and knowing he had not been wrong about the year I would have, I expected no marvels. Nonetheless, I wrote back to a number of coaches.

I did return to Dr. Brown's office with a simple request: could I play college basketball—anywhere? He had been monitoring my status during the season, taking X rays occasionally, and weekly drawing large volumes of fluid from my knees. He said no new damage had been done, but that until he opened me up, he couldn't answer my question definitively.

"But is it possible?" I asked.

"I won't say until I'm in there, until I can see in there," he said. "But I will say this. I'm convinced, after this season, that you have the grit to come back. You're a tough little cookie, and that's a factor in the possibility."

Once again, I was awash in possibilities. My old enthusiasms tried to raise their heads and return me to the child in the open field. Hemingway's Code volunteered to retreat. A letter from Juanita continued the assault: she would return for the senior prom, and maybe for good. The crowning blow came when my correspondence and subsequent discussions with coaches left me with invitations to visit three universities: Northwestern, Colorado, and Kansas.

I was not prepared for this turn of events. It came suddenly. At times, I just wanted to slap my hands in wonder or tell somebody how good the world was. Those were old feelings, dormant for a year, and restless to flap in the wind.

But I had learned caution, or, maybe, a natural reticence arose. Sometimes experience has a way of settling issues that divide oneself—the body gets rid of thoughts and feelings that don't belong, and balances those that do. Maybe enthusiasm and persistence were a part of me, but so were fear and anger— even destructive rage. I had to live with it. These characteristics, in tension, were mine, and their various alignments would govern my internal constellation. What shots the external planets would take at me were beyond my knowing.

In the last three weeks of my senior year, I discovered how completely alienated I felt from those who looked back. My present and future consumed me. With Juanita at the senior prom, I blocked off all talk of losses or victories, pranks or problems. In a long, velvet, strapless red dress, with her black hair draped to her shoulders, she walked among the revolving lights and danced past all stares as though she were a law of nature unto herself.

I knew the whispers: "What keeps those two together? How did they keep it going all year? Not me, baby, not in my senior year." I didn't know. Nothing in my self-absorption had contributed to it. Our lovemaking was fumbling and passionate, but not the center of our relationship. Absence didn't make the heart grow fonder, but we didn't threaten to leave or find someone else. We stayed together, perhaps, because we were growing up separately, not crowding each other with our adolescence. We had time apart to grow, and, finally, after struggling, get pleasure from our progress when together. We were a surprise to ourselves and each other.

I was surprised, too, by my three visits to college campuses. At Northwestern, I spent more time with academic counselors than with the coach. What were my plans? What major would

I declare? Study hall was mandatory for athletes. Let's take a tour of the library. At Colorado, I was whisked out into the mountains to look back on campus from the top of a rock. Around me was an unbroken fusion of nature and the university, an awesome sight. I was sure I could live in a tent, carry a backpack, and play basketball at the same time. At Kansas, housed in a fraternity, I met a varsity player first, who suggested we get some of the brothers to play a pick-up game. The veil was thin, and I knew I was being tested. This was a try-out. Later on, I met Wilt Chamberlain, who smiled and asked, "Can he pass the ball?"

I had no idea how to be recruited, nor what I should say about my knees. I knew if I were a coach I wouldn't touch me with a long pole. What good is a playmaker who can't run, twist, split the middle, pass blind on a fast break because he's soaking in the whirlpool? What good is a lob pass in the training room? My knees didn't give out in the mock game at Kansas, and I got on well with the coaches and players at Northwestern and Colorado. I was a month away from the operation that would last four hours, leave me in hard casts for three weeks, strung up like beef, and then pushed, shoved, bent, dragged, squeezed, and stretched into jerky for five weeks. In sum, it wasn't until the end of the summer before I would step back on a basketball court to see if the doctor's now cautiously hopeful analysis of my X rays would stop laughing in the light.

I did not know if any of the coaches would offer me a scholarship, or if my knees would be ready if they did. I did not know if I would be in Muncie next year with Juanita or on a campus far from home. I sometimes imagined that I would get offers from all three universities and have to make a choice. I checked for letters regularly, and then, as the summer passed, I was afraid to open the mailbox. I found that waiting to find out so many things simplified so many things. Who I Would Be gave way to Where I Would Be, and that was like a familiar hand closing one music box to be able to listen to another.

Phil and Tom. "Growing up, I would tag along with my brother, three years older than I, to the . . . baseball field for shortstop practice."

Catherine Raisor. "One year she was elected the national vice president of Alpha Omicron Pi sorority."

Floyd Raisor (left), with his younger brothers, Kenneth and Omer. "I told him I'd once found a helmet in Uncle Om's closet . . . I'd held it up as an archaeological find. Uncle Om wouldn't talk about it."

Tom Raisor (#30) celebrating one of his two state championships. "His letter had reached me the week before: 'The thrill of that first championship is unforgettable and unexplainable.'" Photo courtesy of the *Muncie Star-Press*.

Muncie, Indiana. "Combative and defensive, Muncie built its own history, stealing only what it needed from the world's to make sense of itself." Photo courtesy of Ball State University.

"We'd always stop at the Walnut Street bridge, and nod slightly, a bit apprehensively, at the icon of the city, Chief Munsee."

"John Casterlow walked on a high wire." Photo courtesy of the Delaware County Hall of Fame.

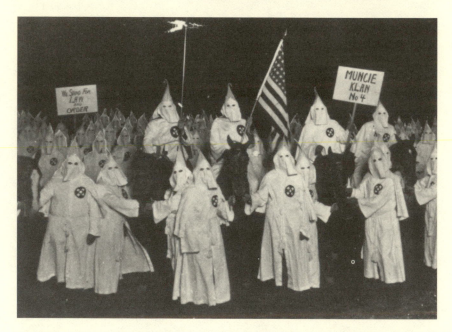

A 1920s picture of the Ku Klux Klan marching in downtown Muncie. In the 1950s, "in Muncie, I noticed no blacks ate at the Elk's Club, where the Purple Gang had lunch. Why would John never join us?" Photo courtesy of Ball State University.

Butler Field House, 1954. "The night game was set—Milan vs. Muncie for the championship." Photo courtesy of Herb Schwomeyer.

Jim Hinds (Muncie) reaching for Ray Craft (Milan). "Craft cuts straight down the middle for the score . . ." Photo courtesy of the *Indianapolis Star*/Maurice Burnett.

"On that immortal night, I slumped down near the foul circle and waited for things to clear and the postgame ceremonies to begin." Photo courtesy of the *Indianapolis Star*/James C. Ramsey.

Juanita Waln.
"On this first full day together,
we relaxed into friendship.
Silence and watching were as
much a part of our conversations
as were words."

Reverend Chester L. Rees.
"Her smile was evanescent. 'I'll bet it's
your grandfather,' I offered. 'Yes,' she
said. 'The best thing in my life.'"

Juanita, Carolyn, and their mother. "I listened to her talk about her . . . life with her parents and sister, twelve years younger than she was."

"She was from Muncie, a majorette in the Central Marching Band . . ."

1955 Bearcats on the road to the "Dream Game." First row,
from left to right. Eddie Collins, Tom Curtis, Jimmy Barnes,
George Burks, Fred Scott, Phil Raisor, assistant coach Carl
Adams. Second row. Coach Jay McCreary and son, John
Casterlow, Gene Flowers, Jim Hinds, Bob King, Dave
Saterfield, Bill Tinder, principal Loren Chastain.

Oscar Robertson and John Casterlow start the second half of
the "Dream Game." "The two of them went at it. I mean it
was personal. They used all the tricks. . . .Sometimes they
were so close at the rim, they looked like one body."

Sometimes during the 1956 season, I'd
start out one way . . . and end up another.
Courtesy of the *Muncie Star-Press*.

Phil, Floyd, Catherine, Tom,
prior to leaving for Kansas
University. "Still, my brother
had flown the coop, and now
I had. We all expected that for
any future trips, we'd have to
come home, realign, and
adjust to changes we had not
seen taking place."

Kansas University, 1957. From left to right. Ron Loneski, Coach Dick Harp, Wilt Chamberlain. "Wilt was surrounded by incredible talent." Photo coutesy of the *Lawrence Daily Journal World.*

Fred Scott and Juanita Waln, 1957. "I had to write Juanita that I wouldn't be able to attend her senior prom. . . . Juanita said she understood. Scotty was in town and would take her."

Beta Theta Pi house. From left to right. Dave Hanna, Fielding Norton, Jack Kollmann, Russ Boley. "I saw in them the makings of another Purple Gang." Photos courtesy of the University Archives, Kenneth Spencer Research Library, University of Kansas Libraries.

Tom and Martha (Marty) Chappell at the University of Michigan. He wrote me that she was "a splendid girl, trim as a white pine, stable as an anchor, and bright as a Lake Douglas sunrise."

LSU against Mississippi, 1958. "No one needed to explain
anything to anyone as we watched Billy Cannon slip and
slide, break six tackles, and run the length of the field."
*Gumbo Yearbook,* 1959, © Louisiana State University.

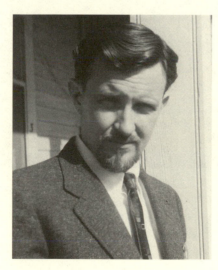

John William Corrington,
1960s. "It didn't take
much for me to see him
in a Confederate uniform,
but I knew he would cor-
rect me. 'I will fight for
the life of the black man
and his freedom as much
as I will my own.'" Photo
courtesy of Joyce Corrington.

LSU against Vanderbilt, 1958. "The *Advocate* newspaper story the next morning pointed out that 'The Commodores dominated the backboards completely.'" Gumbo Yearbook, 1959, © Louisiana State University.

Juanita and Phil.
"We didn't expect much. A walk on campus, a dance,
a movie here and there, a couple over for hamburgers—that was all the time, or money, we had."

Bernard Benstock. "He seemed to all of us to be a true mentor, both leading and listening to discussion, encouraging us all." Photo courtesy of Shari Benstock.

William Mills. "Billy stepped into another one of his skins, another set of his eyes. He became sharply focused and rigid, as he calculated where he would enter and where he would exit."

Spring, 1960. Students from all-black Southern University. "Against the advice of their president and many of their parents, a half-dozen leaders organized sit-ins, marches and boycotts which for a month rattled the whole fabric of Louisiana society." Photo courtesy of the Baton Rouge *Morning Advocate.*

"If they were not served, if they sat in terror, the movement, I was told, was theirs. For now, my help wasn't needed. Their black arms on the countertops is what they wanted the world to see." Photo courtesy of the *Morning Advocate*.

Juanita and Staci, 1960. "My dreams for me didn't stop when we got married. They didn't stop with this child. I want you both in my life, and I'm not going anywhere. But this is my mind and my body. I give them both to you. But I keep them, too."

# 5

# Heartbreak Hotel

Kansas. What do you think of? Land flatter than Indiana's and hardscrabble farmers in the dust bowl? "Quantrill's Raiders" and towns torn apart by marauders? One of the free states? Where Dorothy lived before she found herself on a yellow brick road? Or maybe even Kansas City jazz with Kansas City steak? Instead, try thinking of a small ice cream parlor in a small college town where weary travelers could shake off August heat and thank God they made it. Not even the thought of a plunge into the Kaw River was as refreshing as that peppermint topped with marshmallow sauce.

The trip from Muncie to Lawrence, Kansas, was not unlike the ones we used to take to the Michigan woods, but our packed car seemed smaller, tighter. More bags, more books. Tom and I were taller, filling out, and I had less space to gesture, punctuate my points, especially holding a desk lamp on my lap. In the front seat, Mom and Dad seemed to listen more deeply and talk more as though time, no matter how hard it tried, could not dislodge them from the center of this family. Still, my brother had flown the coop, and now I had. We all expected that for any future trips, we'd have to come home, realign, and adjust to changes we had not seen taking place.

Maybe that's why, during a stretch between Indianapolis and St. Louis, Dad held forth about our family in Muncie, America, and the first half of the twentieth century. A wry, serious, meandering tale of immigration, Midwest settlement, farmers and factory workers, athletes and educators, and women who held it together. I wanted to know about bootleggers, bandits, our California connections, and the two great-grandfathers, who, steely eyed in their opposite Civil War uniforms, stared from portraits at our family reunions. Dad wanted to talk about going from dirt roads and outhouses to cement highways and in-house plumbing, from no radio to that godawful Elvis. Tom, born in 1935, pushed him for more details about how we fared in the Depression. I pushed him for more about World War II. I told him I'd once found a helmet in Uncle Om's closet when we were building that addition on his house. I'd held it up as an archeological find. Uncle Om wouldn't talk about it.

Dad looked back at us. He must have figured now was an appropriate time to tell a brother's story. "Om told me about it once," he said. "He said he'd only tell it to me and later to his son. It was during the Battle of the Bulge. The snow was freezing; they were trapped on a hillside. They caught a German platoon sneaking behind them and captured them all. What could they do? They needed every man and rifle. A couple of our guys lined them up in two columns and marched them off."

I was thinking of Mailer's *The Naked and the Dead*—the Crofts of the world, maybe anyone.

"Twenty minutes later, his guys came back. Your uncle was standing there as they passed. One of them handed him the helmet. 'A souvenir,' he said. The blood was already dry."

We sat silently for awhile, and then Dad said, "I wasn't surprised. That's a picture of all of us creeping out between the cracks. I hope you two boys," he said, "can come out of college with different ways of doing things. God knows we've been brave, but we've screwed it up too."

Lawrence was smaller than Muncie. I realized immediately, though, that I was no longer thinking in terms of size. I was thinking in terms of expectations. Only four full basketball scholarships had been given to freshmen, and two of them had been given to Indiana boys—Bob Hickman of Terre Haute and me. We would play in Allen Field House, a spit-polish new (1955), top-of-the-line stadium with a seating capacity of seventeen thousand. Dr. James Naismith, who invented basketball, had brought his brainchild to Kansas in 1898, then later turned it over to Coach Phog Allen who won a national championship in 1952. Now, with Wilt Chamberlain here, news reporters crammed the bleachers at practice trying to extract the strategy that was sure to win another one.

Wilt was surrounded by incredible talent. Maurice King, Bob Billings, and Ron Loneski were Big Seven All-Conference players. Everybody was high school All-State. Even players passing through to see Wilt brought amazing skills. One Saturday I was shooting around at a gym. Wilt and a guy named Elgin Baylor bounced in. Baylor was headed for Seattle University. He was about 6' 5", 225 pounds. His moves were like air— swirls, dips, flows. They wanted me to pass from angles, loft the ball high, so they could bang on the boards against each other. Wilt blocked hard, broad-legged; Elgin anticipated flying elbows and slipped underneath. At first I was simply the launch-pin, the arm that sends the clay pigeons into the eye of the shotgun. Then we all got into the game. They leaned into each other only to break quickly when the ball bounced off the rim or slipped inches beyond their fingers. One-on-one Baylor would drive on Wilt, change the ball in the air from one hand to the other, lift it near the net, only to have it slapped away. "Above the rim, Dipper, you're above the rim!" Elgin would shout. Wilt, laughing, would say this wasn't Seattle-ball; this was Dipper-ball.

Another day after practice Wilt bumped me in the back, picked me up by the seat of the pants, jiggled me, and said, "You too skinny. Git in the weight room."

I agreed. But I hated weight rooms, just as I hated long-distance running. We did neither in high school, but I was quickly learning that no one here cared about high school. The day Wilt walked in I was struggling with 150 pounds, trying to bench press it. I was concentrating very hard, and paid him no mind. I grasped, not grabbed, the bar and drove my whole body toward the lift. I was a pulley, an assembly line, an escalator. Up the bar came, up the weights came, four inches, eight inches, I was getting it to my shoulders, then my eyes, then . . . the sonofabitch felt like a fixed wall, then like it was crumbling, then I dodged just in time. A barbell falling on a cement floor has a particularly horrendous hollow thong! that brings laughter. No one looks; everyone knows what's happened.

I was prone on the bench, and way up there Wilt hovered over me, not laughing, but slightly smiling. "You doin' it wrong," he said. I shrugged at the obvious. "Here's how." Wilt dried his one hand and wrist and wrapped a towel around them as though he had a sprain. His forearm was larger than my bicep flexed. He stretched his fingers out of the wrapping, jiggled them (I thought a bit too dramatically), and then palmed the bar, with one hand. "Now, Mr. Razorblade," he said. "What you think about is putting this little twig . . ." and as he riffed on and on, he slowly lifted the weights past my stomach, my eyes, and to the top of his reach somewhere up in the damn skylights. "Now, puttin' it down is like a leaf falling, oh, so softly in a light breeze." "Yeah, yeah," I said, heading toward the shower, listening to his chuckling behind me.

None of the coaches ever asked about my knees—how they felt, how my rehabilitation was going. I didn't know what all the coaches knew, what the trainers, news reporters, fans-in-the-stands knew; it all seemed a large, secret society. I supposed most freshmen players at Muncie Central probably felt the same way upon entering the hallowed world of the Bearcats, but since I had been pulled early into that enchanted land by my father and brother, I found this network of inaccessible thinking and conversation a new experience. One thing was clear: conditioning was mandatory, guided by a long sheet of expectations and reinforced by a bevy of overseers.

We ran miles over the campus golf course, and more miles around the Field House, lifted weights, stretched the deltoids, tightened the soleus. We expanded the lungs with windsprints and rolled over and over on the ground for God-knows-why. Once my knees began to swell, gnarly and full of juice, the trainer called me in. He looked at the pale red scars and asked how long ago had I had the surgery. Then began the twice-a-week aspirations; I would sit on a cold metal stool while the trainer drained each knee with a long needle and syringe. In the past year in high school I had become accustomed to this procedure, anticipating the moment when the needle would reach the exact spot where the excruciating pain would occur. Now, I surprised the trainer by joking with him at that moment we both knew could not be joked away.

I sensed a change in the coaches' response to me, but I had no idea if it had to do with my knees. Though it passed my mind that *maybe* they had not known about my surgery, I was more concerned with what they didn't like about the way I played the game. During the first weeks of practice, I ran the court, shot, and passed the way I always had. Then, I began to hear from the freshman coach. He told me to dump the two-handed set shot. When he had to tell me the second time, he told me to dump my butt on the bench until I understood. I understood quickly, accepting that it was all jump shots from here on in. Then he yelled to stop the damn dribbling. "We want passes. Passes. They get there faster." All right, it's passes from here on in. So I passed. Then he came out yelling that if he ever saw another behind-the-back pass, he'd take both arms off at the sockets. "We want straight-forward, two-handed push passes, got it!" I got it, I could learn, but I wondered why in the hell they had recruited me if they didn't like the way I played. I also learned that slow learning got me twenty-five wind-sprints, so there went the knees again, water slushing around in a toilet.

Although in the late fifties freshmen could not play on the varsity, we did practice with them, usually in the role of the upcoming opposing team. We were the green shirts; they were the black shirts. Since the coaches could not get rid of all of my contortions, they used it. I would be the opposing guard most like myself, if there were such a creature. I could play my game as a green shirt, so that they could show how a stolen pass or excessive dribbling could get the black shirts an easy lay-up or a faster break. But I was expected to play like the black shirts during freshman intersquad games, prior to the Jayhawks' packed-house battles against Oklahoma, Colorado, or Kansas State.

At least by the end of the freshman season, I had managed to make progress toward the coaches' expectations. Although my knees should have improved more than they had, I had learned the habit-of-mind that excluded two-hand set shots, pulling up too far behind the foul circle, or passing blindly on a fast break. Coaches Harp and Waugh seemed pleased with my technical improvements. Even in the *Daily Kansan,* the editor wrote a column I could clip and send home to my father. In talking about the team's prospects for next year, and who might play where, he wrote that for the guard position,

Raisor has the offensive edge with a fine shot off the jump and a nice floor game. He displayed some of the fanciest passing

seen on the Allen Field House floor this year with his demonstration in the freshman intersquad games.

However, he must correct defensive troubles if he is to gain a
starting nod, but with an outside shooting guard a must, he
could have the edge.

We suggest a line-up of 5-11 Billings, 6-0 Raisor; 7-0
Chamberlain; 6-4 Loneski; and 6-4 Donaghue as maybe the
starting KU team for next year and our choice for the Big Seven
Championship.

I quietly made copies, and then walked softly among my teammates who might not have seen the same arrangement for
next year.

The highlight of my first year came when the Jayhawks
advanced to the final game of the national championship in
Kansas City, Missouri. Wilt had gotten us there as everyone said
he would. As a group, the freshman team drove forty miles
down to the Municipal Auditorium in K.C. We sat on the rows
behind the Jayhawks, and watched them, in the afternoon,
shred San Francisco, the 1955 and 1956 champions, while
North Carolina stumbled and fought to a three-overtime victory
over Michigan State. At night, movie stars, radio commentators, a hundred journalists, 10,500 fans, and, for the first time,
a national television audience for an NCAA championship
game joined together for what *Sports Illustrated*'s senior con-
tributing editor Frank Deford would call, in 1999, "the greatest
college basketball game ever."

I kept seeing myself in the game; I couldn't help it. I was not
a very good fan—keeping apprised of the score, picking out
the enemy to hate, ranting at my own players' stupid passes,
believing my will could change the outcome. Nor was I the
trained journalist looking calmly for my lead and the details to
nail it. I was moving inside Bob Billings's mind and feeling with
Wilt the sharp blow on my knees from a cheap shot and even
the hair jerked from my thighs. But Carolina didn't get a 31-0
record by only being pests. Rosenbluth, Quigg, and Brennan
outrebounded our front line, and Maurice and Billings couldn't
hit from outside. Dipper was squeezed like a peanut butter
sandwich. Tight man-to-man and zone defenses on both sides
frustrated normally relaxed shooters. Elbows got sharper. Ron

Loneski slammed the ball down after missing his deadly, soft left-handed hook, and then fouling. Wilt spat words at Quigg. Coach McGuire yelled at Coach Harp. Twice players grappled at the center circle. Once Coach Waugh had to shout us back to our seats as we started to join the melee on the floor. No one scored in the second overtime. No one could hold a lead. No one, until Joe Quigg sank two free throws and then batted away Loneski's pass to Wilt in the final seconds.

We lost 54-53. Milan and Attucks all over again. I felt myself drift right down into the middle of the hole. Would it never go away? Did each new loss reaffirm its existence, collect all the debris from past losses that strengthened its walls? In 1998, less than two years before he died of an apparent heart attack, Wilt told a crowd of thirteen thousand fans, who had come to Allen Field House to celebrate the retirement of his jersey, "Forty years ago, I lost a heartbreaking battle, the toughest loss of my life, to North Carolina by one point in triple overtime. It was devastating because I felt I had let KU down." I watched Wilt walk off the floor in 1957, despair in each of his steps. Even then I knew our worlds would be different, but for one moment, whatever came afterwards, I knew he had been tracked by Wayne Klepfer—he had been where breathing and the blood's flow would never be the same.

Still, on the way back to Lawrence, I began to watch the world around me and smell the leather gloves I held close to my nose. Headlights passed us, but even the traffic was slow. I had never noticed before a billboard advertisement for a Holiday Inn. Gradually, I turned away from Jim Hoffman's commentary on the game in the back seat, and remembered how the ride back to Muncie from almost all the losing games was the same. Then, when I started thinking about Juanita and my family, I realized I was planning ahead. I had gotten one game closer to being on the floor where I could ask them to be my guests at the final game of the national championship.

I figured the odds were in my favor now. One of these days, for the big game, I was going to be on the winning side. One day!

My first letters to Juanita in September were frenetic outpourings of odds and ends—*Kansas,* "KaNze" meaning "south wind," a Sioux word I learned on a windless day, a cow-town feeling, the steep slant from downtown to the campus on top of Mt. Oread; sandstone buildings and fountains; the "whiteness" of the whole area, and the day I saw a black person refused lunch; a beer blast on Saturday night with an endless keg; the first week of fraternity "rush" and, then, already, already, the sense of incompleteness I felt in not being with her.

We wrote regularly at first, and then intermittently as our schedules allowed. Juanita said she would seize the day—good grades, a scholarship to Ball State if possible, live in one place for the whole year, be a good friend to those who had kept in touch with her when she was away. Her mother worked in an office at Warner Gear; Juanita filed papers part-time in a medical clinic. Still the beauty queen and sterling majorette, Juanita said the loss of either would not disturb her. She had always been forced to live in the moment, building self-esteem by an act of will. Now, she was hoping her will would be stronger than any moment. The senior prom, she said—our going together—would be the only crowning glory she needed for the year.

I realized, then, the power of familiar places. All last year, in vacant tracks of time, I had brought Juanita back to Muncie. She was probably tacking up posters on a bulletin board at Howe, but, in my mind, her fingers stroked my arm at Goff's Restaurant or her hand flipped back her hair at Tuhey Pool. I could cross Ashland Avenue or mow a lane of grass in my backyard; she would join me. We walked down University Street, over by Faris's house, toward White River. Now, that past threatened my present. Here I was in a maze of wide sidewalks and flat-headed buildings. I memorized street signs, then forgot them. I entered hallways, then lost the entrance. When Juanita appeared, I had no place to take her. She floated like a dust mote in the eye. I wrote letters for comfort, but felt they were going back to the past.

Juanita was shocked, elated, troubled when I strode into a Muncie Bearcat basketball game on a Friday night in the first week of the season. I had hitchhiked the six hundred miles from Lawrence. No one knew I was coming. I waved to her among the majorettes as I walked up the steps of the gym to sit with my stunned parents. We watched the first quarter in silence. I could feel my father's anger. A sixteen-wheeler, two teenagers who roused a drunk at a stoplight, a couple who threatened each other for forty miles, and a truck driver who told me, as I stepped from the cab, he'd held a .38 on me just in case, had brought me back to Walnut Street, a hamburger at Orv's, and the Muncie Field House. I wanted nothing but a weekend, a day and a half, to grab the past and force it into my present. Somehow, I thought I could settle my new land that way. Juanita couldn't stop laughing. My mother joined my father in reminding me that I had an athletic/ACADEMIC scholarship at KU, and where were my books?

On Monday, I returned to Lawrence (Dad coughed up bus fare) and the Beta Theta Pi House. I had pledged the social fraternity during rush week, a time when everyone in a house was my friend and mentor. "Would you like some coffee? My girlfriend's got a girlfriend. I'm especially close to Professor Rodriguez for Spanish 102. You'll see, the guys in this fraternity are absolutely terrific." I was told by the Betas that whatever I needed to concentrate on basketball and my studies would be supported. Besides, they said, your brother is president of the chapter at Michigan; imagine yourself in three years, here, at Alpha Nu. Why not? My pledge brothers would be new friends Russ Boley, Jack Kollmann, Dave Hanna, and Allen Forker. I saw in them the makings of another Purple Gang. "Hey-ho," we sang till 2 A.M. at the Wagon Wheel,

> Let's grope the girls, hey-ho
> and shout the Phi Delts down,
> and when they rise to sing,
> let's spread the farts around.

"Pledge Training" began the week an upperclassman leaned into my face and explained how I was a stupid, mindless *keesh.* Twenty of us, the pledge class, were herded into the cleared dining room and stripped down to our shorts. We were told our mere existence desecrated the honor of successful alums who supported this brotherhood with their money and souls. We weren't worthy of their worst dreams. We were slops. I looked around for boot camp buses and military uniforms.

One night, after a two-and-a-half-hour basketball practice, I headed straight for the geography text in my room. On the first quiz, I had gotten a B-. I knew where Madagascar was, but I didn't know that the major passes through the Bering Sea were Unimak, Tanoga, Amukta, and whatever. For tomorrow's midterm exam we had to map the path of the Amazon River through the Brazilian rain forest to the Atlantic Ocean. That was an all-nighter, a couple of No-Dozes. The pledge trainer came sniffing around, and found I had slipped Juanita's picture out of my drawer and onto my desk. He started pounding on the floor. Five upperclassmen swarmed into my room, stared at the picture as though they were watching an autopsy, and then bombarded me with epithets, demerits, threats to my genitals, and castration of our first-born. I hit the floor, but twenty push-ups were not enough. My pledge brothers were called out to witness my violation and punishment. Down to the dining room we marched. Down to my shorts. Down to the floor. "Fifty this time, you miserable *keesh!* Crawl, you slop, you legless pig!"

The next morning, I walked out of my room, and the PT, smiling, said, "Hey, Razoo, you need a ride up the hill, I'll get you one." Around the corner, Boley, Kollmann, and Hanna, up there hooting with everybody else, started the usual joking. Another day. Last night forgotten. I couldn't. I walked to class, expecting to flunk the exam. My knees were logs. Everybody, I thought, needs to tear somebody down so they can build them back up in *their* image. I sensed this was partly self-pity, but more as well. We had been studying the poet John Donne's Holy Sonnets in English class on Tuesday. He had one about a sinner begging God to purify him:

> Batter my heart three-personed God; for you
> As yet but knock, breathe, shine, and seek to mend;
> That I may rise and stand, o'erthrow me and bend
> Your force to break, blow, burn and make me new.

All right, I thought. This sinner says to blacksmith God to hammer him down, break him apart, and put him back together again. All right. God can do that. But what business do we have doing it? Where's the democracy in all that? Where's the family? I heard Scotty—*"Dig deep. Dig to the bone."*

Toward the middle of the second semester I had to write Juanita that I wouldn't be able to attend her senior prom. The whole pledge class had been locked down that week and no escapes for any reason were allowed. I tried death in the family, cataclysms in Indiana, everything. No escapes. Either stay or get out. Juanita said she understood. Scotty was in town and would take her.

The night of the prom I sat in a dark, cold room lit only by a single candle and listened to a progress report from my peers: "Listen, Razoo, a muffled 'screw you' instead of a loud 'Yes, Sir!' is an inappropriate response for a *keesh;* so is not attending group study. And why aren't you more like your brother? Where's the Rock Chalk enthusiasm for this fraternity? Are you listening?" Sure I was, of course I was, I said, as I watched in my mind, poor twinkle-toes Scotty mis-stepping his way on the dance floor, following Juanita's graceful lead.

Three weeks later I moved from relief and humorous invention to terror:

April 9, 1957

Dear Juanita,

I wondered why I hadn't heard from you for awhile, but now I guess I know. Last night I got a call from a mutual friend in Muncie. She was breathless to tell me the latest gossip. I love gossip, don't you? It brings out of the woodwork all the giddy fears and tremblings of the gossiped-about. Gossip wreaks havoc, transforms illusions, and laughs its ass off on the way to the party. I'm not laughing. I'm sitting here like waste in a lab, wondering who will sweep me up.

How do I ask my girl, the love of my life, future wife, how do I ask why she and my best friend are out-about-the-town, secreting themselves in corners, staying out, say the late night Mickey Spillanes, until two and three in the morning? Are they talking about me, about us, all the time? What problems do we have that he's solving?

Your faces change in front of me. I see Halloween masks, corporate czars, things without feelings.

You and Fred have every right to do whatever you want. Hell,

I probably could figure out, better than anyone, why you would come together at this time.

I sit here and realize I've been inside the Garden of Eden all the time, naming animals and plants and running around shooting baskets and holding on to a departed rib I still thought was mine.

What comes next? Explanations, I guess. But you and Fred aren't on trial in my courtroom. I'm not judge here. I've got fifty push-ups to do, a term paper on Malraux's *Man's Fate,* and a breaking heart to deal with. That's enough.

                                                            Phil


                                                April 18, 1957

Dear Juanita,

I got Scotty's letter. I got your letter. I got Scotty's phone call. I got yours. I got supporting data from the Purple Gang and the Marching Five-Thousand including Drum Major. All say that so-called friend is a lying bitch and drunk and jealous—and why didn't I know or sense or suspect or reject every piece of lying trash she told me. Yes, it's true that Scotty and Juanita have gone out a few times and that he took her to the Prom and they've had a couple of dates afterwards, but that doesn't mean anything's going on. You've got to have patience, you've got to have trust, and both of them right now are going through some pretty tough times, and you're not here. You'll never have a greater friend than Scotty or a greater girl than Juanita, so if you'll just look at it from all sides you'll see that neither one of them could hurt you intentionally.

Tell me now. Was it that good of a Prom?

I wouldn't know what's true and untrue out of all of this if I had a screen to separate the wheat from the chaff. My heart says believe those you care most about. My head says the same thing. But deep down, deep down. And that lying bitch, as far as I know, has always been a pretty decent person.

The other day, a week ago, I stood on the Kaw River Bridge. The sun and breeze said that winter is over. I saw the bark relaxing on the oaks, the world around me loosening, untying belts, letting the gray clouds sift higher.

In my world, though, I could hardly breathe. Coach Harp had called me into his office. He said he wanted to talk about next year. He said I had every gift he needed; yes, I could make the traveling squad, even start for the Jayhawks. But he still wasn't sure I fit in. There was something about me he wasn't comfortable with. He told me to work hard over the summer.

I got to the Beta House, and the PT called me in to say that he wanted me to think very seriously about whether or not I wanted to go through initiation next month. Some of the upperclassmen felt that I was, perhaps, temperamentally unsuited, that I showed an attitude not really seen in pledges before. Maybe I wanted to reassess my commitment. Maybe . . . well, would I think about what I thought.

And then I thought about you. How very little I really know you. I thought I did, and not because you would open up about what you thought and felt. I just thought I did. I know you've got good reason to have tons of anger buried in you. How does that get out? How do you get back at your father, at your situation? OK, maybe I'm way off, but I would never have even asked those questions before.

I've got to tell you. I had this thought. I've been reading Albert Camus in this philosophy class. I even got an A on an exam about his *Myth of Sisyphus*. He says that in our time, "There is but one truly serious philosophical problem, and that is suicide." I'd gotten my A, but never felt his thinking had anything to do with *me*. But Now, Goddamn it! Now . . . maybe the whole universe is nothing but a big hole!

Aw, hell, what do I know? What do I know?

I do know this, though. I can't know what you and Scotty have or have not done, and believing or not believing you simply buries the other side. So I'm going forward, not knowing. And I want you and Scotty to come with me because what I do know is that I care for you. To stomp on that is to stomp on something real inside me. And I'm not going around kicking myself anymore. I've been there.

As Always,
Phil


April 25, 1957

Dearest Phil,

You don't understand. You don't understand at all. You see details as though each one glowed clearly in a dark room. I see them always as in pale light. You hear Fred and I are out late. You think only one thing. We're doing something. You've been betrayed. That's all you see. But for me, on those evenings we're out, I see laughter around a table. I hear a story—you never told me—about silly boys chasing pigs, sloppy, silly, wonderful boys. We talk in the *front* seat of the car about how hard it is to be without one's father and how deep the wound feels sometimes. You couldn't understand. I don't blame you. You've just never had that experience.

You're right. I do have anger in me, but you don't, can't, understand what I do with it. I think I was born with it; at least, every time we've moved, it rises, and that seems like it's been forever. Yet, no one's said to me before, "Juanita, your anger might make you betray me." I take that's what you meant. But you're wrong. I've always taken my anger and used it. I've looked in the mirror time after time, and when I see it rising I know what it looks like when it gets to my face. Do you think I've ever wanted that on my face?

You've got to understand.

I take my anger and use it. I make things out of it—interior decorating, the way I dance, even the way I get between friends who don't know how to control their anger. Right now I'm angry. Right now, you're afraid. If we can't run away from either, who do you think's going to handle it best?

That's what I mean by pale light. You're always in front of me as part of all I do. But you're not there alone—either as a shining star or some big ogre. You're just part of all I live in. I live in spaces where sometimes there's nothing, sometimes great anticipation, sometimes I need friends to talk to. Fred's a dear friend.

Don't make too much of this. Please, darling, don't make too much of this. And please, for God's sake, don't ever go near the Kaw River Bridge.

Love,
Nita

We settled into an impasse during the last month of the semester, realizing nothing would be resolved until I got home for the summer. I concentrated on not quitting—Juanita, the fraternity, school. Around me, my pledge brothers sensed the time was near, the end of initiation, full membership in Beta Theta Pi. The final night of pledge training was one I would remember—the taste of raw liver, coated with flour, blood seeping then squishing down my throat, the angry shouting, a carousel of distorted faces swirling by me. I did my push-ups, recited my lines, was honored to be honored, and, with songs and cheers resounding all around, hugged my brothers, all, in joyous exultation. I had my pin. I looked around to smash the pledge trainer's face.

I knew that next year I would concentrate only on basketball. I tried to remember one practice this year when I had been fully consumed by it, when my sweat felt like basketball sweat. When, I asked myself, did I feel that my body and the air and the shouting and the screech of rubber on the floor and the whole flow of the running and the starting-and-stopping, when did all that transport me, really transport me? Not once—not even close. I set my sight on being one fiery Jayhawk on practice day one.

But for awhile, there would still be Boley and Kollmann and Hanna and Forker and the Wagon Wheel, where we could sing and celebrate, each for his own reason, the end of the first year of college:

> We'll sing with the geese, hey-ho,
> And drink with the cows in the barn,
> Until the pretty girls walk by
> And leave us dead on the lawn.

At times during the summer, I felt my father watching me, as though sand was drifting through his fingers. I told him I had been reading Karl Marx a good deal, and found socialism an exciting experiment. He said that was a bunch of crap. I said my real problem with China and Russia was their oppression of the individual, and their invidious influence on a dumbass like Senator McCarthy who didn't even know he was using their tactics for the same purpose. "What in hell's name are you talking about?" he shouted. "This is America, young man. What are they teaching you in that school?" I told him it had nothing to do with Kansas, that I was really enrolled in the University of the World.

I didn't know yet what I believed, but I enjoyed the spark of ideas, the sound they made as they zapped another idea, or fell of their own lack of volition. Besides, I was tired of watching "You Bet Your Life" or "Father Knows Best" at dinner time. A reference to Fidel Castro, the Suez Canal debacle, or the Hungarian Revolution would always turn down the TV and turn up the heat on the day's headlines. I really didn't have much connection to my classes and professors yet, but I knew I should bring book knowledge into my life as well as my brain. I wanted more than one moment on the Kaw River Bridge to feel that what I read at KU would deeply influence my choices.

Environment continued its impact on our lives. Familiar surroundings rekindle familiar feelings. At least, when I got home, Juanita and I began a reconciliation that led back to the last time we sat on the hood of my father's car and hashed out all the reasons we should never marry, and then decided it was inevitable. That was last summer, but during the first three weeks of my return from KU, we met accidentally at Burkie's Drive-Inn, Haag's Drugs, and Woolworth's. Then, we started talking at Orv's and the bleachers overlooking the Bearcat football field. In July, after a long afternoon of swimming and tennis at Tuhey's, we watched city league softball under the lights and then returned to Dad's old Plymouth.

We didn't talk about Scotty, or Beta Theta Pi or basketball. We talked about having our own car together, a joint checking account, getting the best deal on used books ("Oh, yeah," she laughed. "I'm going to Ball State this fall; my parents agreed on something. They were able to get tuition by selling the sweaty lining of my majorette uniform to a dog biscuit company."). I stepped into the moonlight, in my shorts and high tops, and showed her my Elvis routine. After laughing, she was conciliatory, sympathetic, understanding.

"I'd heard," she said, "that you suffered from St. Vitus' Dance. I'm sorry."

"No, no," I said, thinking of the Beta House. "That's my 'Heartbreak Hotel' rendition."

She suggested I keep my day job and thought meditation might help.

Only once before we knew we were back together did we go very deeply. "I will want your time," Juanita said. "I will want you close to me. I don't care what you win, how big you get, but I will want you there." I understood that in one brief moment, we had covered all we had not talked about.

I returned to the Beta House in August. Now a full-fledged member, I entered quietly, got the warm and secret handshake from my four pals, and dumped my bags in a third-floor room. I knew I would be looking for an apartment right away. Over the summer my sense about the fraternity had clarified for me, since I spent a good deal of time thinking and reading. I enjoyed being alone. Others enjoyed the camaraderie of large, traditional programs whose ideals they shared. Churches, corporations, policeman's balls, baseball games, military units, and bee colonies were, so to say, gatherings of Betas. I realized that I, too, sometimes admired the unity and competition within communal groups, hence my attraction to socialism. But I also knew that my most intense feelings were generated by the single image of a child on crutches, one light in a tall building, Bob Feller's fastball, a Matthew Brady photograph, a mannequin in a window, or watching one ant until it disappeared in the mass. I realized my disaffection from the fraternity came as much from my own inclinations as the stupidity of hazing.

I did, however, find one ritual compelling. Pinning. It was a lesser commitment than an engagement, but still an active step toward marriage. The wildest celebrations erupted when a sorority and fraternity could toss a Saturday night bash in honor of two of their own who had been measured, linked, and approved by gossip and mandate. I was sure that was the process that had led to Tom's pinning to Martha (Marty) Chappell, an Alpha Delta Pi at Michigan, who he had made special to me by describing her as "a splendid girl, trim as a white pine, stable as an anchor, and bright as a Lake Douglas sunrise." Now that Juanita had enrolled at Ball State and was planning to rush for a sorority, we began to discuss this route as a commitment we could make to step beyond our troubles of last spring.

A month later, when I told Coach Harp I was pinned, he congratulated me. When I floated the idea that we might want to get married in the next year or so, he didn't. I said I wouldn't be asking for more scholarship money, that Juanita would be in school and work part-time. I said we'd take out student loans, the Stouffer Apartments weren't too expensive, and all sorts of people had offered furniture. He stared at me, as though irritated I would bring up the subject. He said the basketball program had a policy. The policy was that none of its players would be married. I saw brick and mortar rising straight out of the ground, stacking up row after row.

I don't know when I began to sense that enthusiasm, a well-trained body, and sharp focus on basketball might not be enough to trip the wire that would explode me into fame.

In early November, my father took a play from my book, and surprised me with a visit. At practice one afternoon, I saw him sitting alone in the stands. He told me later he just wanted to see how I was doing. I figured Coach Harp had contacted him. What my father saw, he said, was a pencil drawing of what I had been. My moves were mechanical, I passed the ball with a starched arm, I stayed on the perimeter like a stick-in-the-mud. I wouldn't be playing for Kansas at this rate. He didn't need to tell me. Even if my knees were still slowing me down, I realized I had not made the adjustment from the free-wheeling independence instilled deep in my bones and Coach Harp's locked-down patterns.

That night, at a large diner, Dad and I waved to Wilt and a couple of his black friends, laughing and gesturing, in the corner. I knew how hard he had fought in Lawrence to break an implicit and pervasive segregation. He had even threatened to leave the Jayhawks if one more damn owner refused any black people service. The word spread, and no one dared. I pointed to my father, mouthed "my father," and introduced him in the air that stands still for one moment as people move past each other in crowded spaces. I spent the evening trying to pry out of Dad the history of the KKK in Muncie. He spent it trying to figure out how I could quickly adapt to Coach Harp.

The next day, after my father left, I walked toward Allen Field House knowing what I had to do. I had to play my way or I was dead. Just the thought of the scramble, the toss off the dribble, the wrist-flicking lob over a forward I'd frozen like a scarecrow, energized me. I could only hope it worked, that a blind pass to a Billings back-door cut would leave him wide open. I knew there was no room for mistakes.

Halfway through practice, Coach shuffled the line-up. I was playing with Loneski and Chamberlain. Twice, I cut down the middle and flipped it high for Wilt to lay it over the rim. He winked back. Then when Loneski made a great pick I swirled behind him, picked off the guard, and fired a behind-the-back pass from just off the floor straight at Wilt firmly balanced in the pivot. It smashed him in the face. "Goddam it!" he yelled, his hand reaching for the blood slipping from his nose. Both Coaches Harp and Waugh leaped to the floor, one to Wilt, one to me. I got Coach Harp. "Son, I don't think. I just don't think you'll ever . . . ," and his words trailed off.

He sat me down. After the scrimmage, Coach Waugh started some defensive drills, two-on-one, full-court press. I was still sitting. Then Coach Harp called me out. He wanted me to try something. I was to come over the center line and park in the left corner. John Cleland, our toughest defensive man, would be ten feet from me. I was to pass the ball into the foul circle. Use the two-handed push pass only. Get it by Cleland between his kneecaps and his shoulders. Don't bounce it near his feet, don't one-hand it past his head. Cleland knows what's coming, and knocks down everything I try. I'm trying to throw a basketball through a baseball strike zone he's standing in front of. For ten minutes, Coach Harp kept saying "Do it again. Do it again." Everything stopped, everyone was watching. Everyone was getting more and more embarrassed for me. He was asking me to do what I couldn't do. I asked him to let me change places with John. I'd knock down his attempts for awhile. "Keep passing," he said tonelessly. At the end, when Coach Harp had had enough, he looked around and shook his head, pursed his lips, and dismissed me to the locker room.

I'm sure no one was surprised to hear I wasn't on the traveling squad to the Oklahoma State game the next week. I knew Coach McCreary had taken the job as head coach at Louisiana State University the year after Jimmy Barnes and I graduated, so I called him to see if he'd be interested in my transferring there. I could hear the delight in his yes he would. I told him I wanted to get married. He asked who. I said Juanita. He seemed even more delighted, and said he'd tell Mary, his wife.

The disappointment reached beyond my family into Bob

Barnett's column in the *Muncie Star* announcing my departure from KU, and finally to Juanita. I think her first months at Ball State were exciting for her in ways the unsettling and disruptive years in high school could not have been. On a large campus, among a widely diverse student body, stimulated by classes and parties and endlessly different conversations, she must have made discoveries about herself and what she wanted that surprised even her. Here I was throwing in another disruption, another throwback to remind her of what she had hoped we could leave. Yes, we would plan to get married in Louisiana, but where was that, would it ever happen?

I wrote Juanita about my departure from KU—the last night's blizzard, seventeen thousand screaming fans packed in Allen Field House, the Jayhawks winning again, and my long train trip to Baton Rouge, the smell of sewage rising from the Mississippi River, the 950 fans watching like pallbearers while "we" lost for the tenth time. I said I understood though that football was big here. Maybe we'd win a football national championship.

I remember three weeks later picking up Juanita's letter from my mailbox in the Huey P. Long Field House, and walking to a bench near a billion-year-old tree, covered with Spanish moss, next to a billion-year-old swamp. I watched a squirrel cavort in the leaves, the same squirrel the world had always known, yet one that had a scar across its nose and a distinctive tail wag.

I felt a lump in the letter, and knew what it was.

Strangely, a calm settled over me. No, I was not in control of anything. I could hold on to nothing. I was no more than one insignificant piece in an enormous, incomprehensible puzzle, and that, watching the squirrel disappear, seemed all right with me.

I sat back to watch motion and unmotion all around me, forming already the sentences I would write to her. I would say I will imagine you in botany class, sweeping aside objections, and insisting that the cilia-like hairs on paramecium are best understood as rudders not oars. I will see you in a sorority driveway pasting paper ringlets on a Ferris wheel float you will grace the next evening as queen. I will see you taking half your check from the clinic to help pay your mother's bills. I will not see you where I don't want to see you.

I slipped the pin from the envelope and tossed it into the murky water.

She needed time, she said, she needed freedom to discover who she really was.

All around me nothing moved, nothing but the rapid pace of my mind which stayed deeply in the past, until I accepted gratefully each nuance of pleasure, anticipation, pain, and sadness that had held us together. Yet, I now understood that when eighteen says I need to go, nineteen says, yes, love, I know, I know.

# 6

# *Aprés le* Mardi Gras

Maybe it was the begonia's rush of color on the Louisiana State University campus or the contours of the Greek Theater near Tiger Town, but I had a thought that was both fresh and ancient. I would drift for a while, recover, start anew. Occasionally that spring of 1958 I attended classes, shot some hoops in the gym, and took in a few Fellini movies, but mainly I wandered around, absorbing the Spanish architecture and the creaking and slapping sounds of the Mississippi River. Only once, sitting on a bar stool in the Unicorn Bar and Grill, did I grind away at my failures the previous year at Kansas University. I had blown my chance to play on the Jayhawks with Wilt Chamberlain. I had hated fraternity life. I had lost the love of my life. But a few more drinks and I saw things differently: I had another basketball scholarship and was eight hundred miles from the past. Louisiana had struck me as a wonderfully exotic place where *Herbert* was pronounced *A-bear* and bayous and Huey Longs were not impossible to imagine. Three Saturdays in a row I hitchhiked from Baton Rouge to New Orleans just to be on the road. It wasn't as hard as I had thought to tell myself: "Get on with your life. Get on with it."

One of the first things I wanted to do was go to Mardi Gras. I'd seen pictures. I'd heard stories. How better to get on, to get down the road, than to cop a disguise, disappear into a festival, and wander raucously through Bourbon Street. Throw away the middle-class basketball player who had had plenty of sunlight and let him come back anonymously. All my life I had been a growing plant in the window, admired and tended. Now, though wilted, I had dug myself up. That's where I wanted to be for now—a root system dangling in the wind. Because of NCAA transfer rules, I could not play on the LSU team until the following January, so I had one year to reinvent myself. Maybe discover myself. On Fat Tuesday I headed toward New Orleans to get started, smelling already the steaming crawfish étouffée.

In the French Quarter, where darkness had been shoved aside, I wandered into the damndest trap. After a Hurricane drink at Pat O'Brien's and a couple of beers at Pete Fountain's, I slipped easily into a snake of people, masked and chanting, who tossed beads up to balconies and caught flowers coming down. Two pale arms slipped around my neck and I was kissed below my own half-mask. Then she was gone. I felt jostled and grabbed my back pocket, but my billfold was still there. A circle formed and I was linked to a skeleton's elbow that spun me into a fluffy cat on stilts that flapped and danced its paws on top of my head. Someone shouted "Boogaloo!" and I guess that's what we started doing. Then I was pushed through a door into a packed bar and a hand was unbuttoning my shirt. "Let's loosen up," a male voice said, and I was kissed again. I jerked away and, pinned between two bodies, caromed against a pillar. I was free, backing out like a gunslinger at a showdown. When a street vendor offered me a hot dog, I laughed and chose a slice of pizza instead. With another beer in hand and another ensemble forming, I joined the revelry for a nightlong dance. I knew no one. I was no one. I was just music in a honky-tonk town.

I don't know why, but the chair you sit in on the first day of class tends to become *your* chair for the semester. Befuddlement always follows any rearrangement. No one who comes in late the next meeting says, "Excuse me. You're in my chair," but a student displaced shuffles and glares and arrives early the next time. Since most teachers are right-handed, I liked being to their left. They'd see me eventually, but not first.

Dr. Bernard Benstock, the schedule said, as I sat strategically. English 55, Modern Literature, 1 MWF, 3 Credits. Dr. Ben Stock. Sounds like a cowboy from Texas, I thought, checking out the faces, sitting postures, and book markers of my classmates. Mainly English majors, I concluded, neither impressed nor disturbed.

I saw Professor Benstock when he walked in, but not first. A stunningly beautiful girl preceded him. She smiled, knowing we were all staring. He smiled, knowing if we saw him, we didn't really see him. Once she settled near the window, and he sat on the corner of the desk, we could all see, with smiles on our faces, that his performance had begun. Professor Benstock was no Texas cowboy. He was small, self-confident, and casual. He wore a light cotton shirt, European jeans, and sandals. Lighting a foul-smelling cigarette (a Gauloise, I learned later) he said, "I attend all classes, except when it rains. I will attend then if one of you will pick me up. I live off-campus, don't drive, don't want to learn. I'm a New Yorker, but don't worry, I love the South—and I also love Paris and Barcelona and all sorts of places. Our stage here has no walls. All are welcome— all sentiments, all forms, all voices. Except when it rains."

We chuckled together, and he called the roll. I loved the names: Dubeux, Cumbo, Bouterie, Terrebonne. There was also a Kane and a Smith, but I was already listening for Plauché, Faucheux, Gasquet. The professor spoke easily, accurately, as though the names mattered. Immediately thereafter he began randomly to call on us. It was clear that either he had a photographic memory or was using a memory trick to pin us down. No hiding this semester. We thanked him though. Her name was Pat. Pat Planchard. We could glance now, secretly, but feel somehow that we actually knew her.

I waited for his syllabus, comments on course grades, office hours—the usual. But his eyes slowly moved around the room, pausing quietly to look at us, in no hurry to move past or see deeply or embarrass us. He had no books. He had no notes.

"You will see in this course," he said, "skeletons with red spots on them, words that dance in black ivy. You will see buildings fall into half-gray pale light. Don't think that the cry of a seagull is plaintive. It is the back door of the wind. I want you to see a character as porridge, not as born in Brooklyn. Try looking at the chair in front of you as a child's scribble. When the great cities fall, when dams give way to thunderous tears, think of Humpty Dumpty. You will say that your father is a mild man, an accountant with a firm in Shreveport. Look for angel's wings, stuck under his shirt, maggoty and dry.

"Our world cannot be seen with the eyes. We do too much seeing with the eyes.

"I know we are born in place and time, but what place, what time? You will be as dead as Zeus is in our time. Count on it. But last night in the song you sang in the shower, the water rolling off your back, in the bare purity of brain and body, it didn't matter. You let in the cauldron of words, words disconnected from the familiar rant, fragments of words, words trying to become yours. We live in the possibility of words, in the possibility of worlds, and nothing is dead but the end of possibility.

"In this course, I simply ask you to live. In and through these works you will read, I will ask you to return to where you have been and see it differently. I think you will find that where you have been is where you are going. Nothing gets lost or left behind in our worlds. See you Wednesday."

The first things I thought as I left the room were that some of this was nonsense, some a disturbingly unique way of thinking, and some of it was a direct challenge to me. "We do too much seeing with the eyes." I had been going around, Dedalus-like, picking out things to see with my eyes, and now I'm supposed to see with what? My imagination? How do I do that? I was walking directly behind Pat Planchard. I tried to see her with my imagination. As what? It didn't work. No doubt about it—she was a model or a beauty queen. Her arms were loose and moved fluidly as she glided down the hall. Under her was a pageant stage. Maybe that was seeing her with my imagination. I didn't think that's what the professor meant, though.

A small group of students gathered her in as they waited outside of Professor Benstock's office. I recognized one as the editor of the *Delta* literary magazine. Another had a cashmere scarf twirled around his neck. All posed, all were on display, but that was what we jocks did as well. Pat was smiling, aloof, as in a framed portrait. Hey, for that, I thought, I would write poetry.

The cafeteria in the Huey P. Long Field House was a maze of bodies. Half of it was filled with fraternity and sorority types and the other half, it seemed, with football players and their fans. I had met the stars Billy Cannon, Max Fugler, Johnny Robinson—All-Americans and future pro players—at the training table. That was part of our scholarship—two good meals a day in the athletes' dorm. Football was king here, and I had left Wilt and the high-powered basketball program back at Kansas.

I wouldn't miss the notoriety. I eased into the crowd of milling students, looking for one open seat.

"It's packed. I mean, not even a ledge. Mind if I?"

"No, no. Sit," he said, not looking up, but placing a fork and salt shaker in a horizontal line with a tightly rolled napkin.

I placed my Coke and paper plate on the corner, trying not to invade his two-thirds of the table. "Mind?" he asked, pointing to one of my french fries. "Take it," I said, adding a couple to my mouth. He squeezed the fry into a circle and placed it opposite to his line. "That's the 'copse of trees,'" he said. Just as I was wondering why he didn't take the last onion ring on his plate and use it as trees, he deftly placed it to the right of the fry, in front of the napkin cannister, and left of a vase with an artificial rose in it. A pen, another fry, and two rubber bands later, he removed his plate to his lap and sat back.

"Pickett's Charge," he said.

"You got ketchup on your coat sleeve," I said.

"Now look at this," he said, lifting and sucking his sleeve. "This is all open space in the middle. The copse of trees here. Cemetery Ridge there. Pickett's got Longstreet's orders to take the Ridge, forty-five hundred troops, Wilcox and Lang on his left, and Pettigrew on his right. He's got to move from here to here," he said, pointing from eraser to toothpick.

"Is this Civil War stuff?" I asked. "Are you a history teacher?"

He slowly lifted his hand and his concentration from the battlefield and stared at me as though I were an invading alien. But his look was mixed with humor, as though he understood I was not a threatening invader, just an ignorant one.

"Stay with me," he said, returning to his tactics. "Pickett charges, a mile and a half line of beautiful synchronicity with four-fifths of a mile to go. Union artillery blasts away gouging great holes in the divisions. They realign, the charge continues, only Mayo's left flank breaks (the little weasel), but Garnett, Pettigrew, and Armisted remain firm. The right flank reaches the Angle, hand-to-hand combat all around, the artillery's still coming in. But where are the reinforcements? We're that close, that half-inch close to breaking through to Meade's fat ass and we can't get a horse for our goddam kingdom."

"So what happens?" I asked.

He sat back, then leaned back in his chair. "You're a Yankee with a Yankee accent and clearly a Yankee education. Didn't you ever learn anything about the War Between the States, Robert E. Lee, the Battle of Gettysburg, and Pickett's Charge on July 3, 1863?"

"Ah," I said. "We had this teacher in American History who was gung-ho on the antebellum South and Europe's role in the Civil War, so . . ."

"So, did you get lost trying to get down to the girls at Fort Lauderdale? Did you take a wrong turn?" he asked, chuckling.

Teaching time was over, but I strongly sensed that here was a man who wasn't living in the past, but bringing the past into the present. He wanted to fight that war again, to replan, add another brigade or two to the battle, write a different outcome. I told him I was from Indiana (he shook his head sorrowfully), had just come in from Kansas (he threw his hands in the air and exploded "My God, a free-stater to boot") and was on the LSU basketball team. He stood up and said, "My name's John William Corrington. I'm a southerner. I teach English. You read W. J. Cash's *The Mind of the South* and come and see me. I'll read up on this basketball thing, and come to one of your games. Deal?" I gave him my name, agreed to the deal, and watched him in his long black leather military coat part the waters of students as he walked.

In the next two months, I nurtured many random impulses and slipped from the clock-time world into one of my own invention. I don't mean I abandoned classes or forgot to pick up my scholarship check. In fact, I became quite sociable, joining the Benstock coterie and polishing my pool-playing skills in Tiger Town. I read Cash's book—the first part of it at any rate—met with Corrington, and was awed at his commitment to construct a new South that didn't dismantle the old one. One day he surprised me by saying that his short research visit to LSU was over, he was returning to Rice University, but he expected, upon completion of his thesis, to join the LSU staff. Disappointed, but buoyed by his self-confidence, I marveled at the fullness of his mind and abruptness of his moves. He was a dynamo both inside and out.

I couldn't exactly see Corrington and Benstock chatting

warmly in the same room, but separately they had unsettled
me, stirred me, and made me walk across campus differently.
I saw the porticos and magnolias, but they danced to my own
emotions and the whims of my own imaginings. In Benstock's
class I was studying some of the Impressionists and reading
e.e. cummings, Wallace Stevens, and T. S. Eliot. I walked around
trying to create the world I was living in.

Pat Planchard fit in, somewhere, I hoped. We went out a few
times, and once while listening to some jazz at the Unicorn,
she had lightly touched the back of my hand, then my neck.
We were friends, possibly more, but I wasn't ready and she was
unreadable, given both to languid, long-gazing looks and indif-
ferent dismissals. But when she floated down the library steps
toward me one afternoon, I saw her not only as the reigning
"Miss Baton Rouge" which she was in fact, but also as a Cubist
painting in a field of Queen Anne's lace. I thought maybe I was
starting to understand what Benstock was talking about.

Nothing had changed. Coach McCreary was still the affable,
basketball-obsessed man who had difficulty remembering why
anything else mattered. Yes, he and Mary were sorry to hear
that Juanita and I weren't getting married, but that would free
me to concentrate on practice and recruiting. "We need players," he said. "LSU has been the doormat in the Southeastern
Conference since Bob Pettit's days, so we've got to get people."
I understood what that meant. Getting "people" wasn't just
recruiting talent. I had been on winning and losing teams, and
had seen and played with and against some of the finest talent
in America, but building a team was getting people together
who could think, understand, and accept their roles together. I
had not been able to be one of the "people" at Kansas, but I
was expected to be one of the leaders here.

One afternoon, after practice, and after watching us stumble
through the same patterns we had used in high school so suc-
cessfully, I followed Coach to his office. "Why don't we go get
John Casterlow?" I asked. "I hear he left Ball State. I'll bet we
could get him." Coach McCreary had no pictures of his family
on his desk, or photographs on his walls of championship teams
in Muncie (a mix of black and white players), or any of his col-

lege degrees or coaching awards. He had only mementos of former LSU teams. His office was small and bare. He shuffled a few papers, pointed for me to sit down, and asked if I liked it here so far. He said we'd have to have a tighter three-two zone, and that on the fast break we needed to get the ball to the center-man faster, faster. He asked if I saw many, or any, negroes on campus.

I would learn later that LSU was one of the first universities in the South to open its doors to black students at the graduate level, but I told Coach McCreary that, no, in my undergraduate classes, even in the more than two hundred students in my sociology class, there were none. I told him the story about the professor who walked in the first day of my class and said he had three biases that influenced his teaching: he loved athletes, he loved ROTC students (being a former military man himself), and he hated nigruhs. I expected a reaction from Coach, knowing how supportive he had been of black players at Muncie Central. "What'd you do?" he asked. I told him I'd left the class, and he turned slightly aside with a pained expression. "What?" I asked, surprised. He looked down at his shoes, a gesture I'd seen many times. It announced that he was uncomfortable, that the words he was going to say reached beyond basketball into territory he didn't like to enter. "You might want to be careful with what you say and do down here. This is Louisiana, not Indiana." I told him that in some respects I didn't see a whole lot of difference, but he had made the point that he would not be recruiting John Casterlow or any other black players. I remember thinking, as I left his office, that neither one of us belonged in this room and that, perhaps, Coach McCreary already knew it.

But basketball sometimes feels like a creature, a living thing, maybe a she—seductive, brazen, and entirely mysterious. Once she gets in your bones, she meets your wishes or fears wherever you turn. But most of the time basketball reflects yourself. In the game you can be energetic and heroic, but also confused, passive, submissive, or monstrous. You can out-think your opponent, and be stupid the next second; you can be totally self-absorbed in a hot streak, and totally bonded with others in a loss. Family, religion, and politics are never absent from a game. Compressed into brief moments, a move your father taught you, a prayer for God's help, and a whole cheering section waving placards can provide instant security. A missed jump shot in the last second, on the other hand, can isolate you from yourself and others for weeks. And always, the rules, the form, the time of the game challenge you to define whoever you are. But neither player nor fan, winner or loser, wants to give it up. We—those of us with basketball in our bones—know that it is not life, but neither is it just a game. Like all rituals and myths, it is for believers.

During the last month of the semester, in luxurious early mornings, I dribbled out of my sleep onto a black-topped junior high school court with nets on the rims. Alone, uncriticized, unadmired, I loped and spun and dashed like a rabbit still alive after hunting season. Normally I hated wind-sprints and stand-in-place-pumping-knees routines, but with the sun breaking against shadows I rushed right on through my aversions. I took jump shots from all five points around the foul circle. Over and over I tried to dunk the ball. Dribbling it between my legs and flicking a back-pass on a fast break, I imagined the last seconds against Kentucky. I even created a fall-away shot off a forward pick I knew no one could touch. Deep down is where exhilaration starts, not in playing on the number-one-ranked team, not even in winning game after game, but in keeping alive the sensations and pictures that push the kid into a crowd. I had to find out, and did, that the child was still in the young man.

Some of that spirit carried over into my campus life. I realized I was an outsider, a stranger whose past was not a southern past. But maybe I could be a New Yankee in a New South. I knew race was going to be an issue with me, but most of my teammates were southern born, southern bred, from close-knit families who could and did recount histories of fine, generous people. Marty Broussard, our team trainer, a dark and quiet man in his forties, whose slicked-back hair made him look Italian, taped ankles, probed groins, and carried the wounded from the field. But his manner said he was a gentleman from an old school, where grace and cordiality, even in the midst of bloody faces and violent games, were not to be ignored.

I knew that was true. Decent people are everywhere, and I wish I had read Cash's study of the southern mind all the way through. I would have understood much more about the complex world I had entered. But I was in the "collecting impressions" stage, more concerned with juxtaposing images and people than analyzing them. I had just gotten here. I wanted to stack the deck. Over here are the racist types, but, look, over here, how many more Broussards there are.

It didn't work that way. I had learned that Indiana had a racist history which was subtly affecting its present, and there were still some Quantrill's Raiders parked in downtown Lawrence, Kansas. But in Louisiana it was open season on the beast, yet so mixed up, you couldn't always tell who was the hunter and who the prey.

I remember one night watching Earl Long, the governor of Louisiana, on television. A supporter of racial segregation, Long would carry candy in his pocket so that when a black person reached to greet him, he could pop a peppermint stick in the black hand, rather than shake it. Yet, he was a prominent supporter of health, education, and welfare programs aimed at assisting black citizens, and he increased black voter registration threefold during his term. A crafty politician, he improved the lot of poor blacks while increasing black support for himself, but he had to take some severe hits from white supremacists.

On this night I was sitting on a stool in Woolworth's in downtown Baton Rouge watching Governor Long go crazy. None of us could believe it. For months we had been following Ol' Earl's escapades with New Orleans stripper Blaze Starr that had led to his wife's very public humiliation. He didn't seem to care, so she didn't seem to care either when she had him declared insane. Since he wasn't, he said, and wanted the people of Louisiana to know it, he got air time to tell them that his wife, keepers, state police, half the Louisiana politicians, and the family who had Huey killed were crazy, and even the judge who had to decide on his sanity was a crazy ol' son-of-bitch. I saw poor King Lear on the side of a hill, raging into a storm, baring his broken soul.

Above the mirror over the counter a sign read "White Only."

I asked the waitress if that meant what I thought. She frowned, and turned back to wrapping silverware in napkins. Only whites were at the counter. A few black people were back in the aisles, all riveted to Earl's ranting. I asked the waitress why they couldn't sit up here. She looked, not at me, but at the woman on my left and the man on my right as though I had surely offended them. She motioned to the manager, whispered to him, and I saw the word "Looney" directed at me. He came over and said quietly that seating arrangements were national store policy, and he would get me the home address if I would like to write headquarters.

As I walked from the all-white counter, I passed a black man with distinctive white hair and a clipped mustache. He was clearly a man who was used to holding doors for people. I knew he had overheard my question to the waitress. As I left, he held the door open and stared at me with all the scorn he could muster.

In his last farewell harangue, as we sat at the Unicorn, Bill Corrington, restless and unfaltering, pushed me to mingle and listen to *all* the voices of the South. "Read Faulkner now, not tomorrow, now," Corrington said. He said I would have to learn, and Faulkner was a good place to start, "that we're not all about race, not all about loss. We're also about change and human decency." But the one thing foremost on his mind was what connected him to the Old South. We should be left alone to do what we want. Within the frame of human decency, "no one should damn well tell me what I can or cannot do," he would say. "I will die or kill for that." It didn't take much for me to see him in a Confederate uniform, but I knew he would correct me. "I will fight for the life of the black man and his freedom as much as I will my own. By human decency," he would say, "I mean human decency for us all." He left on a train that night, carrying his various promises like a badge of honor.

I knew one thing. I was a Yankee, in the middle of serious southern business, and had no right to make judgments. I liked some voices I heard better than others. But it was clear they were all mixed up together here, and had been for a century or more. All I wondered is: are they talking to each other? I knew from my fraternity and basketball experiences that there were all sorts of systems out there which could keep that from happening.

Occasionally, Dr. Benstock (Berni outside of class) invited several of us over to his apartment for a collaborative gourmet dinner. We all pitched in, and under his instructions, chopped, marinated, sautéed, combined, sprinkled, served, and then talked late into the evening about all matters that touched upon the intellect. The talk was mainly literary, though, including the writing of stories, poems, and plays. Sometimes, Pat read a favorite passage from Joseph Conrad or Bob Prentice took a section from Thomas Mann. No one was surprised when I read "To an Athlete Dying Young," but they cut me off after a few stanzas of "Ode to the Confederate Dead." At times, Bob and I competed for Pat's eyes. Hers seemed to fall more often on Berni's. We weren't jealous. He seemed to all of us to be a true mentor, both leading and listening to discussion, encouraging us all. "You might want to read Hugh Kenner on that subject," he would say. "Yes, Phil, I agree with what Corrington says about the people and values in Faulkner, but look at his use of myth as well. Look at not only what is said, but how it is said." Jimmy Naremore was a burgeoning film buff, and when he spoke we would turn to new films for the next hour. I remember thinking, walking to my dorm room, that maybe I could be a writer, scholar, maybe a teacher. Then, before falling off to sleep, I would make a couple of jump shots and see my name on the roster of the Boston Celtics.

Usually on Tuesday and Friday afternoons, sometimes Sunday mornings, a mixed breed of the Benstock group would meet at the Pepper Pot in Tiger Town. We would take up space in the corner, order coffee, and lounge. Rafe Kellog, a large, robust man from somewhere in Pennsylvania, was the owner of the small restaurant and the pharmacy connected to it. He was a huge fan of Tiger football and basketball, and, standing among his aisles of purple and gold teddy bears, alligators, tigers, and streamers, he would shout hellos and attaboys as though he were on the sidelines. When I walked in with Wayne Monson and Joe Combs, my teammates, he'd back-slap us all, but when I was parked at a table with the literati, he'd shake his head and look away. Once I saw him mockingly curtsy as we thumbed through his new paperbacks.

"Hey, kid," Kellog said one Sunday morning from his perch behind the prescription drugs. "You want to go to a party?" His smile was sly, conspiratorial, as though he knew for sure I'd want to go to this one. Barbecue, beer, a bunch of other jocks, and God knows what else—at his place this afternoon around one o'clock.

The last time I'd hung out with the jock mafia was at what turned out to be my initiation. Two weeks into the semester I was shooting pool one night at one of the bars on Nicholson Drive and a guy burst through the door, breathing hard and gesturing. "She's down the road, banging again. Come on." Maybe it's because on any team we're all trained to move simultaneously or because we don't want anyone to get a step ahead of us that we rush forward like lemmings. In the car I was told this beautiful chick would periodically screw football players while her husband was trucking somewhere in California. She was insatiable. She was like a monkey. She'd wait down the dark road and flick the headlights when she was ready for the next one. Drop your pants when you're in the headlights, yell that you're a linebacker, and dive into the back seat. Oh, you won't believe it!

I had my hand on my buckle in the middle of the road, pushed thirty steps ahead by those behind me, when a shotgun went off, and a guy leaps into the headlights firing at me. "You son-of-a-wife-fucking-bitch," he yells. I didn't wait. I dove straight and hard to my right. Immediately I felt the swamp water suck me in, vine leaves flap at my face, and snapping jaws clack at my shoulder. Another shotgun blast and I swam twice as hard. I was groping for a tree when a ring of headlights zeroed in on me and I heard the laughter split the swamp wide open. "Welcome to Tiger territory," someone yelled, and the laughter began again.

For awhile my nickname was "Fast-Break" and my penance was to listen to the story over and over. The initiation was short and painless though—far removed from the prolonged humiliations of the fraternity world at Kansas. But when I started hanging out with the Benstock group, and someone stuck up on the training room bulletin board a poem I'd written, I found some of the guys had difficulty talking with me. Then, when word got around that I had been asking about the possibility of recruiting black athletes, I heard that one football player wanted to know why the shotgun hadn't been aimed at my nigger-lovin' ass. It was a strange feeling surveying a weight room and wondering which one, or how many, wanted my pelt strung up in a smokehouse.

I told Kellog I'd make his party if I could, but I had final exams to bone up for. He laughed and said, "Oh, yeah. I know what's on your mind." Not likely, I thought, but he couldn't stop laughing, so I headed toward the library. After an hour of Middle English, two hours of authoritarian dictatorships and despotism, and a quick review of the amoeba, I started back toward the dorm. On a whim, or maybe because I wanted distraction, I decided I'd head for Kellog's backyard.

As I walked across the LSU campus, I watched myself walking—outside of myself as I sometimes did, as sometimes I watched my mind thinking or quietly rollicking toward its own absurd connections: a horseshoe ringing a strawberry sundae in the middle of a salmon run. Fun stuff. Stuff that let me walk now like a Confederate soldier toward a reunion of veterans of Corrington's favorite Siege of Shreveport. My stride was ungraceful, broken by a limp, a shrapnel wound. Across the lawn, in front of the Memorial Tower, cadets marched under an arch of sabers. They saluted me—man of manliness and honor. Mike the Tiger, LSU's mascot, paced in his cage as I passed. How could I not strut in his presence. I did. Then I felt the bars collapse on me in a deluge of, what was that coming down? Ah, spaghetti. "The grave's a fine and private place, / but none I think do there embrace." Thank you, Miss McCormick, English 50. I wondered when that would be useful. I saw General William Tecumseh Sherman, LSU's first president, escaping from his portrait in the library. I rode with him, an angry subordinate, singing the Muncie Central Bearcat fight song. At the football stadium, an oracle, surrounded by sixty thousand dancing and shouting sorority girls, made this prediction:

Since you are not what you seem,
You will be seen as not what you are.
Be ready to become what you will be.

As usual, with this nonsense, I had gotten somewhere. I was going to tell Coach McCreary something. What was it? Oh, yes, I'd talked to John Casterlow. He said he knew about the South from his momma. One side of him said he'd rather kiss a dead body in a grave. The other side said he wouldn't mind marching down here to kick some ass.

Walking up Kellog's driveway toward his back door, I was laughing and believing I had, in fact, arrived at the world Berni Benstock wanted me to see.

"Come on in, kid," Kellog said, just as I started to knock.

I had seen only two cars parked in front, and none of the jazz or rock 'n' roll I expected was coming from the backyard.

"I'm either late or early," I said.

"You're the main dish, my man," he said, opening the sliding door. "Once you're here, the flies will gather."

I was surprised that Kellog's house, a ranch in suburbia, wasn't larger. He knew how to make the impression that he was a man of means, but his kitchen was small, vinyl, tacky yellow, with bar stools at a round, fiberglass table. I could smell essence-of-something and hear, from another room, the clarinet of Pete Fountain.

"Great stuff," I said, pointing from wherever the recording was coming from. He laughed, and said, "Oh, yeah, we got great tubes here today." He walked to the refrigerator, where a fan wheel was grinding slightly, and said, "We got wine, beer, cokes, vaseline, whatever you want."

He's not good at stand-up comedy, I thought, as I settled down on a stool. I noticed a Chinese lantern hanging in an archway, and realized that Kellog must have developed a penchant for French Quarter kitsch. A couple of Hurricane glasses balanced precariously on a windowsill, several strings of beads dangled from a bread box, and a white whirligig cane hung on a nail. In the silence between Pete's offerings, I heard Venetian blinds drop and looked through a doorway into a living room. The room darkened briefly and then a pale red light crossed the wall.

"What's up?" I asked lightly, expecting something unusual. Hell, this was supposed to turn into a party!

Kellog handed me a beer and leaned against the refrigerator. I noticed the wheel stopped whirring. He looked at me as though now he would let me see the real, quiet, sincere, serious Rafe Kellog.

Thumping started in the living room, the sound of bare heels on hardwood floors. I looked, he smiled, and I watched two LSU football players, in jock straps only, parade past the doorway and then leap back like ballet dancers. Kellog looked closely at me, rubbing his fingers across his lips.

"Want to join them?" he asked quietly.

"No, Kellog," I said. "I don't want to join them. But what the hell *are* they doing?"

"Come on, Phil," he said. "We know you're a queen."

"Know I'm a what?" I asked, slowly.

"A queen. We know you're a queen."

"What's a queen?"

"Good Lord, Phil. I set this up for you." Kellog's quiet look left his face, replaced by a slight frown of irritation. "A queen. A queer. I know you want to go in there. They're waiting for you. Come on, now."

"You think I'm a what?"

"Come on, Phil, we know what you are."

"What in the holy hell makes you think I'm queer?" I shouted.

"Now, now, don't get pissed," he said. "I know it's hard. But these guys, you know them, they'll keep it quiet. For Christ's sake, those faggots who hang out with that little faggot professor have kept it quiet."

"So that's it, you dumb sonofabitch," I said.

The red light went off and feet hurried from the living room. I stood up as Kellog's body tightened, his natural instincts working quickly with his apprehension. He saw me rise, and I felt my body fill with the fear and rage so familiar to me now. Klepfer was in my face, and the punk kid at Yopemika. And now Kellog. You don't like my looks, you're a wimp, you're a queer. You're what I say you are, and I'm going to bludgeon it out of you. I knew what a queer did, but I didn't know what a queer was. And this bastard didn't know who I was. So decisions had to be made. His was simple: call for help or not. Mine was complex: I wanted to bust Kellog with an ax, but I did not want to get stomped, dragged, and dismembered by a halfback and a tight end.

In a bizarre thought, I also realized I wanted to get back to the Benstock group to see if I could stop laughing long enough to tell this story.

The feeling of laughter stayed with me, and though I didn't laugh in Kellog's face, I let it calm me. I was learning. I wanted nothing from him, and he couldn't take anything from me.

But how could this happen? I wondered. I tried to see me as Kellog did, a queer disguised as an athlete, hiding from the world and myself. I couldn't see that, any more than I could see past Kellog's face and motives to what he was. What about the jocks in the other room? What brought them to this game? Were they queers? What was a queer anyway except something I was not? Let queers define themselves.

Amazing. Just because I hang out with artists and poets and intellectuals.

But there had to be more than that.

I gave Kellog a hard look as I walked past his rigid body. "Here, asshole," I said, pulling the white cane from the wall and handing it to him. "You sure as hell need this."

My walk back across the campus was filled with misgivings, and then resolve. After today, I knew I would be a target. *Maybe that was it, I thought. Maybe I've been a target all along. Stick on me the label of nigger-lovin' queer, get pictures, and they've got nothing to worry about. I would get packed back to Indiana and never wear an LSU uniform.* But even if not that, Kellog and friends had been rejected. I would live in a more dangerous world now.

My days of drifting and anonymity were over. I would, in fact, have to see with more than my eyes. Benstock was probably right: "Our world cannot be seen with the eyes."

But I felt, as well, that it was time. I had found mind and books and people and issues and place as exciting as basketball. When I heard Corrington talk about the New South, I knew he wasn't envisaging a coalition of Yankees and Rebels who would ride in the night. These guys, this Kellog and klan, were still raiders. I knew Corrington wanted an open South, full of possibilities, a place where walls had fallen down, where northerners and southerners could discover what both had lost.

Ahead of me was the mossy cement of the Greek Theater. I

decided to stop and watch a play. It was a warm afternoon, still bright, with the smell of begonias drifting from the back of the stage. The chorus came forth in its masks. If we must have masks, I said, your instructions are to remove them, one by one. Leaning back on my elbows, lifting my face to the sun, closing my eyes, the play began: *two frogs were dancing on a barrel of poison ivy and along came a jar of asparagus from Natchitoches who was a cousin of Stonewall Jackson . . .*

# 7

# The Hangnail

Louisiana moss, Mississippi dust, Tennessee mud, and now Indiana dandelion parachutes stuck to my banged-up, one-way rental jalopy that barely got me from Baton Rouge to the outskirts of Muncie. I was coming home for summer vacation, not sure why I wasn't staying on to make good money in a Sash and Door warehouse, but I was drawn to a last summer reunion with family and friends. Scotty had called to say we had some friendship rebuilding to do, and he was sure Bob King would be around, so let's get together right away. I was feeling that Muncie would always be my hometown, but I really didn't expect to live here, and I thought that growing away from it was probably right for me. I was excited by the South, and wanted to see more of it. I wanted to play in the NBA. I wanted to hear not only Cajun French but also Parisian French. Brazil and porticos in Spain widened my eyes and imagination. I was ready for a final fling in Muncie, but hoped it wouldn't last too long.

During the previous semester, I had thought of Juanita often, but always in one way. She was still an important part of my life, and she was as fixed in my memory as Milan or Attucks, Yopemika or the Michigan woods. I could replay whole conversations, smell her perfume, and even reconstruct the rhythm of her laughter. But always she was in the past. I didn't dwell on her or hope to reopen our quiet place. I was sure I wanted to see her during the summer, but only to feel happy for her, know that she was in college, had a better home, a new relationship—to know that she had moved on.

Nothing had changed at my parents'—nothing. My brother and I came and went, but the two-story, two-bedroom, one-and-a-half bath with den and eat-in kitchen house was, as it always had been, clean, freshly painted, neatly landscaped, and wide open to visitors. The patio, where spring could turn to fall without a moved glass canter or a new bug trap, was flush with lounge chairs, hanging plants, and a view of the beautiful rose trellis. When I rang the back doorbell, my mother was wiping her hands on a towel and my father was just turning off the desk light. They hooted, and both met me with hugs before I could get my bags through the door. Every piece of furniture was in its usual, unaltered spot. I was indeed home, my mind's favorite place, and the only thing I never wanted changed.

But I had changed, or, at least, I thought I had learned to experience life differently. My sense of time and space was certainly more cluttered, and my perceptions were more angular. I could still see a tree as a tree, but I often let light and shadows rearrange what I saw. I also let my imagination have freer play. A thing was only a thing the way I saw it in a particular state of mind. Since I remembered clearly Berni Benstock's injunction "to return where you have been and see it differently," I had waited for this visit to test it. What did he mean by "I think you will find that where you have been is where you are going?" Was that nonsense or a road map? I knew that I had brought LSU and Baton Rouge along with me for the summer, and I was even surprised how easily that fit in with Berni's conclusion: "Nothing gets lost or left behind in our worlds."

The morning after I arrived my father and I drove around Muncie. I knew it was his way of keeping me in touch with our world. He showed me new stretches of decaying buildings and remarked on the years they were built. The decline of the Ball Brothers plant, an international glass and box company, was an occasion for reconstructing family history. "Your grandfather came from Louisville, Kentucky, in 1902. He worked there over thirty years. During summers, when I wasn't teaching, I worked in the box plant. Hot and stuffy as an old barn. Tom, I think, liked the assembly line his two summers. He'd like a bear pit. Let's see, you had the morning shift in the glass house, or was it in boxes?"

We passed my grandparents' house, which I had not seen in two years. Someone else owned it now. It was a ramshackle mess in a deteriorating neighborhood. I said nothing, remembering only family reunions and tennis and horseback riding in Heekin Park across the street.

"Now here on the north side," Dad said, "Ball State keeps growing. That's good and bad. Property values are up north of Riverside. They're down east of Light Street, where student rentals are taking over. Absentee landlords. You know what kids will do when the cat's away."

I attached my own stories to the places we passed—where I crashed my bike into the oak tree, hit Tom in the eye with a rock, crept to a back window to watch Toby Sue undress. The Ball mansions still arched around Minnetrista Boulevard. We used to pedal our bikes past them on our way to the city golf course. Great wealth and spooky windows went together, and gardens in backyards with dead bodies locked in mausoleums. We'd always stop at the Walnut Street bridge and nod slightly, a bit apprehensively, at the icon of the city, Chief Munsee. A statue, thirty feet high, the chief sat on a massive horse and opened his arms to the Great Universe. We'd all heard stories about the settlement of Muncie along the White River, and the rise and fall of the Delaware Indians. Hungry Joe, the last of the tribe, was rumored to haunt Old Town Hill or, at least, the white man's bar where he drank himself to death.

Indians in Muncie. I had never really *thought* about them. They were stories, street names, park names, a Dick Greene column in the *Star,* attire for Halloween parties, mascots for football teams, cigar holders, targets for cowboys—a vague ancestry, comically or reverently connected to the present. They had no voice, no significance. I didn't even know who Chief Munsee was.

Since my curiosity got the best of me, I found out. He and his tribe had been small, transient, and left to scurry on their own when the really great leader, Tecumseh, aligned his confederation with the British in the colonial war. Settling near the river, Munsee, spelled various ways, remained out of the fray, leaving no mark on history's landscape of war and peace.

Yet, he sat among us, godlike and muscular.

One evening, after good wine at home, and a dinner of chicken a lá king, mashed potatoes, and apple sauce that left me remembering a hundred of them, I drove over to sit with the chief. Why not? It was a beautiful summer evening, dry, without mosquitoes, and Scotty and King and I weren't to meet until the next night.

I sat at the manicured grass of the golf course, and looked across the White River at the statue, outlined by a dim spotlight, and framed by the Marhoffer Plant on the right and the Ball Corporation on the left, two of the city's most powerful influences.

"What do you think, Chief?" I asked. "What are your thoughts on the subject?"

He didn't say a word. So . . . my questions and thoughts had to become his voice. He spoke of generosity and love, of the existence of the divine spirit in all things, of brotherhood with eagle and wolf. Then he got ticked off. He said his legs were cold, and he wished the pigeons would stay off his head. He asked why kids tried to crawl up to him, interrupting his communion with nature, and what about the dogs yapping at his poor pony? What about the stink and the mold? He said his gaze ran right down Walnut Street to the heart of Muncie, and day after day, he watched dark-skinned people like he was blocked from food barns, and several times, a long time ago, he'd seen thousands of white-robed and hooded marchers stream down the streets. What was going on in this sweet land of his ancestors?

I saw him rise up and slide down to the ground, pacing in circles, patting his rigid horse, tugging at it like he wanted to leave, then getting back up as if that's where he belonged. He settled down, raised his arms again, as they had been, and began to chant:

*Dear Great Father, listen to me now, listen to my plea, listen to the blood of my wounds still flowing. I have no hope. I cannot change. I am a stone of the earth, of the Great Mother who dreamed us all. Help me help them, those winged things, who fly in many forms, whose births and deaths come and go like saucers on the plates of gluttons who sit down and will not share their food. Let them hear my plea to eat together from the same bowls and listen to the joyful noises of the ratty birds when mixed with the squawks of the diamond-eyed ones.*

My pants were wet with dew, and I stood and shuffled free of Old Indian Bonnet. I thanked him, laughing lightly, but still aware that in his past I had found common ground to see things. He seemed real to me now. We had worked together to bring him out of the dry plankton of history into the living stream. At least for me. Remembering Bill Corrington's reprise of Pickett's Charge, I felt closer now to my own history. And more respect-ful of it. Maybe it shouldn't be buried. Maybe a reimagined past was useful.

At the thought, I quickly remembered that I had told John Casterlow I would get back to him about LSU, and hadn't. Oh, yes, I thought, memory brings guilt as well. The only relief I felt came from knowing I was only a half mile from John's house.

I drove through McCollough Park, crossed the boulevard, and entered a dense black neighborhood of small houses and apartments, businesses, numerous churches, and empty, over-grown fields. The area was called Whitely, and the irony escaped no one. In my senior year, I'd been there two times, but even with John, then at Ball State, and with my letter jacket on, I felt the tension my presence brought. Downtown, with my black friends, we would joke, bump shoulders, and make the streets sing with our laughter. Here, a wave would get silence, a nod was ignored. I knew I was in the wrong place, especially at night, and no matter how much I told myself that this was my home-town, that John and Jimmy and Othello and Wilk were my friends, I didn't belong. A moment after I stepped out of Dad's car, I felt a thump at the rear. Three teenagers stepped close and positioned themselves around me.

"John Casterlow," I said. "I'm looking for John. He's a friend of mine."

"This thing worth much?" one asked. He stepped to the front, and scraped a fingernail across the hood. "Cheap piece a shit seem to me."

"I came to see John," I said. "You know him?"

"Everybody know 'im," he said, the spokesman. "Wha fo'?"

Everything he said seemed, and probably was, sinister. I could see myself starting a long explanation, and, in the middle of it, swallowing bloody words. I said, "I'm just an ex-Bearcat, and John and I played on the same team, and we just need to talk."

"What yo' name?"

I told him. He shook his head. I said I understood since it had been a couple of years ago, but I knew John would want to see me.

"Ain't here," one of the other boys said from the dark. "Gone Detroit. Gone las' week."

That was enough for me. Since I expected to see a tire iron or a sudden movement in the dark, I'd decided to take *John in Detroit* as a good exit line. I stepped back in the car, saying I'd get his phone number later on and try that way. I heard a thump on the rear as I eased away, knowing this was all quite real, and knowing my thoughts had been locked on the here and now like a crescent wrench.

Driving away, relieved, I had to smile. Chief Munsee, John Casterlow, and I were all the same. Here we were—Muncie-ites, Munsonians, whatever. This was our town. We had been, and in *some* quarters still were, notable—at least recognizable—figures, and yet we were simultaneously outsiders. Community was an evolving idea here, a constantly shifting matrix of forces and relationships that made life complicated. The attraction of Milan—I always thought of Milan (ironically, at this moment, the Milan Indians) when I thought of John—was its fixity, a photograph of Bobby Plump's jump shot that would never change. He would always be an insider in his hometown. I would sometimes have to watch my back.

In too much of a hurry to keep a diary or journal, I sped into adulthood on the rhythms of a country song: "live fast, love hard, die young, and leave a beautiful memory." Photographs, books, letters, news articles, scrapbooks, phone calls, and reminiscences with good friends all aid in the memory's recapture of a past life lived as if it only had one existence. The further I get away from the early stages, the more I see my life as a series of islands. I usually stir up, and let settle, the muddy waters. Then I see clearly how I got from one place to another. Not with the Hangnail episode.

In the few years just before our twenty-fifth high school reunion, the most I could remember about that trip was that Scotty, King, and I, on a crazy whim, took a mad dash down to

Baton Rouge in the summer of 1958. I recalled vividly Scotty and I circling each other in the moonlight under an enormous magnolia tree. I remembered the significance of the event, but I couldn't recall many of the details of getting there. Scotty and I, I knew, wanted to make up, get back to where we were. He was almost engaged to Dina Eder from Knightstown, who we'd both known in high school. I wasn't with Juanita now. Time heals. The past was the past. We both said *maybe* to that, but we wanted to see.

King had the Hangnail, a '48 Pontiac, whose right bumper hung down like a nail off a cuticle. Bob was bright and abrupt at one moment, playfully dense and doddering at another. He was entertaining, and great to be around. I think the three of us thought that this might be our last trip together.

I began to get the details at two o'clock in the morning, after the reunion festivities were over, after we had eaten, drunk, danced, compared, and wondered in amazement at who had done what. King, Scotty, and I headed toward an old haunt— the top of the visitor's dugout at the Muncie Reds' minor-league stadium, now a skeleton of its former glory. We were the opposite of skeletons, having pasted on our bones a middle-aged spread. Scott had overdone it. King had formed an industrial equipment company in Texas, Scotty had his insurance empire in Indianapolis, and I was teaching at a university in Virginia.

"Sure I remember the trip down to that ol' pisspot city," King said, hanging his legs over the roof's edge, and leaning back against the fence. We had kept loosely in touch, forgotten a lot, but found on this night when everyone was remembering that details rushed back in a wonderfully haphazard way. "Oh, yeah, now I remember that," we had heard all evening long. We also tended to settle back into our old high school roles. "Hand me another beer," said King, "and I'll tell you a story about the time I killed snakes and crocodiles in the bayous of Louisiana."

"If I remember correctly," Scotty said, "you went ape when a chameleon jumped off our apartment wall."

"That was before I knew what the little bugger was. Did I tell you earlier Whitey drank himself to death?"

"You did," Scotty said. "You always tell us things twice. And did you hear, Phil, that Klepfer became a Pentecostal minister?"

"I shook his hand tonight at his table. It's still the size of a tire rim. I said I remembered him pretty well. He said, yeah, he'd thought a lot about me too. I still think he wants to kick my ass, preacher or no preacher."

"What he wants," said King, "is to cut your heart in tiny pieces and feed it to the rats in his rag-tag, little drywall church. Now, you wanna listen to my damn story or not?"

We smiled, hearing Bob's gravelly, twangy voice as of old, and settling into the world of reminiscence where truth is shared but the details get debated. I marveled at how easy it was to slip back twenty-five years.

"Me and the Hangnail's the only heroes in this tale," King said. "And you two minor characters are nothing more than little forklifts. Twelve straight hours down Highway 41, the road at times like a tilled field and you two dead silent or trying to sing like the Everly Brothers, with me and the Hangnail plowing headlong into the black night. Evansville, Nashville, Clarksville—*villes* on and on, and lakes and dams rushing by, and the smell of dead skunks and hog farms and river bottoms, and me and the Hangnail fighting sleep while you two snore in sugartit land. Sleep on, dreamers, and miss the wondrous caverns in Realfoot, Tennessee. Then there was McComb, Mississippi, smelling like an oil pit in a filling station. It was just like you, Raisor, to come awake at the edge of New Orleans, start spewing about turn down here to Bourbon Street, and over there's the Court of Two Sisters where you had to run from Tennessee Williams like a steer loader.

"We get to Baton Rouge. We've been there two days, and I see you been feeding us baloney. Where're the girls for us, where're the jobs in a Sash and Door company, where's the foot-stompin' nightlife? Sure, McCreary gets you a job, but not us, and all we get in bars are hookers hanging down like old curtains. And hot, my God it was hot! Even my thoughts were sweating. OK, so you were the only one who had enough money for an apartment lease. OK, but why one with a ceiling fan that won't stir a dust mote instead of an AC? Tell me that.

"And then there was Jimmy Sue. We're dancing in a seedy bar on—I don't know—some street off-campus, and she leans into me and says she's had it, she's got to get her sweaty clothes off before her pores just suck 'em inside. I like all that dirty-type talk, so we head toward her place with me and the Hangnail listening to her here's-what-I-did-today story. She says all day long she's been in a courtroom, a witness for a girlfriend who got raped by a guy who couldn't stop. Jimmy Sue says she was in her bed when her roommate and this guy come in. They go at it, she says, and it was like watching a porno flick, until her friend stops him cold. Cold as crushed ice. But he grabs her, spreads her legs, and fires away. I'm at his back, she says, pounding away, and he's pounding away, we're screaming, and then he smacks us both and leaves. We tell the judge and jury all this, she says, and the asshole gets twenty-five years and good riddance.

"We get to Jimmy Sue's apartment. She comes back in a thin nightgown. I'm ready to get busy. I hear a creaking door. I pause, but Jimmy Sue says not to worry. It's only her room-mate, probably just wants to see the action, get off on it.

"I've got to admit. I'm a damn liar if I don't. The camera-eye element of all that still excites me. I was hotter than a Texas tamale.

"But I ain't stupid. When Jimmy Sue slipped out of that nightgown, said she'd be back in a second, I split out the front door like a Bobcat free loader.

"So no good came of that either. And by the third week, my pal Philip, you were the only one who had any money. Tight-assed as you were, we were eating beans and twenty-five-cent chicken pot pies. Scotty, the Hangnail, and I were packed and would have been gone had we not run into that faggot with deck shoes, cotton pants, floppy hair, and money, money, money. Maybe it was Scotty the blond-boy that got him, but then I'm a Greek god myself in a T-shirt, so what was it—two, three days—he followed us around, paying our bills, saying we could take a shower at his place, promising me and Scotty a job in a week or so.

"But then you two assholes had to go and spoil it."

Scotty stepped up for another beer from the cooler. The Muncie air and moonlight were no match for King's nostalgia. His trip had recaptured us. But we listened to the lapping of the White River for a moment, as we had done in high school days.

We were in many places at this moment. Still, the adventure was unfinished; a runner was trapped in the base paths, so to say, caught in a run-down.

"Let me take it from here," Scotty said.

"Screw you," said King. "And, Raisor, hand me another one."

"No, really," Scott said. "Phil and I didn't spoil anything. We got some stuff clear."

"And screwed up a good deal for me. Look, the guy was dreaming, out of his league, and somewhere down the line I'd probably kicked his ass, about the time he put his hand on my knee. But, Jesus, we went down there for a good ol' time, and we were having it until you two stormed out of that bar and went circling around that magnolia."

"I wouldn't say we stormed out," I said. "It was more tentative than that."

"Oh, hell, go ahead, Scott. Tell your side of things. But I want a final say here. I just thought of something I'd forgotten for years."

Before he began, Scotty looked over at me, as though he was lowering a fishing line into a deep pool and wasn't sure how far to go. Then, he shrugged as though he would just let it drop all the way.

"It was over the guy's billfold," Scotty said. "Or, more accurately, the money in it. You went to the head, Bob, joking to the guy to come with you like you were two girls. He had passed out on the bar, and you ruffled his hair, but he was wasted. You told us to be sure to wake him up when the bill came. It was going to be a dandy.

"I saw his billfold on the floor, alligator hide, his family seal, I supposed, embossed in a corner. Phil and I looked through it—cards, registrations, a group picture in front of the state capitol, and a note on the back which said *'We now have Huey's imprimatur.'* I looked back to the front, and there was this guy in all white, smiling, his arms around three children.

"Then we came to the money. Signed checks—no amount entered—and new hundred-dollar bills packed thickly and tightly in two different slots. I know neither one of us had ever seen cash like that. I didn't know what Phil was thinking, but I was thinking it was ours. How could I think otherwise? I'd never had more than forty bucks in my billfold. It's different now, sure, but then—you guys don't know, have no idea, what it was like for me. The gnawing emptiness. I'd get enough money for one semester at IU. Then I'd eat cereal, potato skins, and canned carrots for every meal. My grades went down. You don't get it. Bob Wilhoite was ready to pounce. 'I told you, you didn't have it. All along, I've told you that!'

"And here was not just fun money, but next semester's tuition.

"So I started to stick this bonanza in my pocket. Phil touched my arm and shook his head. To him—to you, Phil, maybe it was right or wrong, a matter of right or wrong—but to me, it was a matter of survival. Oh, yeah, I had gone to Baton Rouge to mend fences, to air it all out, get it back the way it used to be.

"But I had this money in my hand. When you reached out for it, to give it back, I knew what I wanted. I wanted to show Bob Wilhoite more than I wanted to show you who I was.

"When you saw you weren't getting it, I guess you figured you'd kick my ass. I know what else you were thinking. Damn I know what you were thinking. If I'd steal this, I'd steal your girl. So you figured now you'd gotten the truth, and, boy, were you going to kick my ass.

"You know, I wanted it too, to get it over with. Even to go our separate ways. Because it was damn hard knowing I hadn't messed with Juanita and you thinking I had. So, all right, I thought, start working those fast hands of yours because this is going to be one hell of a fight."

"Oh, yeah," King says. "It was one helluva fight. I get back and faggoty-faggoty is still conked out, and you two are out in the moonlight like Rocky Graziano and Tony Zale jabbing away, feeling each other out. Then the hands come down, and you keep circling, then up, then down, like you couldn't figure out who was going to flail away first. Then, holy shit, you both lean against the tree, and slowly slump like a couple of tears. I'm in here babysitting our cash register, while you two are out there tête-à-têting. What the hell was that all about?"

I smile at Scotty, and we share the pleasure of knowing something the all-knowing Bob King doesn't know.

I even remember the feel of bark on my back, and the thick shadows thrown by the broad leaves of the great magnolia. Scotty and I had watched, for a moment, the moonlight settling on the Mississippi River. It found spots, curled up, nestled into a pale dimness, leaving wide expanses of the river splayed with brightness. Heavy, gray ships, muscular trawlers, and a showboat casino piped their dissonant music to the shore. We listened. The heat was rising hard off the ground. The air was cooling down. In between a foghorn, a piece of jazz in the breeze, the taint of gumbo, we drew on bits and pieces of our history together to circle inward on our division.

We decided neither of us wanted to kick the other's ass. The only thing that got in Scotty's way, who wouldn't back off from anybody, was his own fear of himself. He'd learned how to risk everything, but not where to stop. He said the money was his if he got away with it. I simply asked him if he would steal from Dina, Bob Wilhoite, his employer, his children. He said he wouldn't steal from anyone who mattered to him. Then he just kept thinking. He worked it out from there. He said he knew that the more people who mattered, the fewer he'd steal from. What if everyone mattered? I asked. Then, he said, that was simple; he wouldn't steal from anyone. Would you steal from yourself? He held up his hand to stop me, knowing where I was going. "I know," he said. "I've got to matter to myself." Then he knew what he was afraid of.

He asked if I thought he would steal from me. With Scotty there, and our *whole* past reawakened, I said I felt he wouldn't.

He asked why I hadn't believed him about Juanita. I told him I had a problem with belief—in anything. At Kansas, I said, I'd tried to believe in coaches, fraternity friends, Juanita, God, the Absurd. I'd tried to believe in me. Whatever I thought to be true, even imagined to be true, never worked out. Everything, me included, crumbled like slate. "You," I said, "were just a part of that."

He asked if I could believe him now.

I did believe him. I knew that now. But I knew I only felt I believed him. The next step—truth is only what you feel—made me squirm. I knew I couldn't work that out now. What surprised me was that I *felt* I believed him. I hadn't done that before. I didn't know where that came from. He is telling the truth, my feelings say.

I realized I had moved a step closer to trusting myself.

As we walked back toward the bar, Scotty handed me our pal's billfold, hesitantly at first, and then with a solid thrust. "Put it back in his pocket," he said. "I'll find another way."

On that reunion night, with Scotty remembering along with me, I watched his face, grown rounder, his hair thinner, and I knew it had been an important night for him as well. If he shook his head at what he was, he was sure of what he had become. At ease, comfortable with anyone, secure and self-possessed, he had clearly found another way.

For me, the reunion night itself was a different time zone altogether. I kept flashing back and forth between Muncie at different times, Louisiana then, Virginia now, our lives before the reunion and after. I saw our one, small problem about trust and belief as a problem arising over and over in the lives of so many people I knew. Everyone seemed to have a portion, and I felt myself cross time and space—into my father hanging from a cliff, my uncle with a German helmet in his hand, John and Oscar looking in each other's eyes. I saw it in a southern farmer staring at his hands and the dry, hard earth, in the black kid quickly glancing back at the cop, in a girl's face, forever framed in my mind, as she screamed over a body at Kent State. Even Leda, in ancient Greek myth, watching narrowly as the swan approached her, got into the picture.

King stood up restless and weary. "Boys, I've about had it," he said, dropping his unfinished beer in the cooler. He walked up and down the roof of the dugout, leaning over to peer into the empty space below. "You've worn me out, but I do want to know one thing. What'd you two guys conclude out under that tree? You're still friends."

I told Bob I didn't think we'd concluded anything. We'd only talked about things. Perhaps, I said, we'd gotten closer to understanding one subject at any rate. When he asked what that was, I realized I could not say the word. I had heard it dismissed so often. I remembered the way Hemingway handled it in *A Farewell to Arms,* as a dirty little piece of abstraction that no longer meant anything to him or the world. So it didn't come easy. But it's what Scotty and I had been talking about, so I said quietly, feeling more southern than I ever had, "I think we were talking about—about—honor."

King turned, his eyes wide open, and with his hands going up, he said, "Oh, God, I'm going to piss my pants if you start up that stuff, and, besides, I been thinking here. With Hinds and Flowers gone, I was the starting forward my senior year. I had a heap of damn points. I scored fifteen, twenty points more times than you did. How in the hell'd you get the scholarship to Kansas and I didn't? I mean, shit, my inside move was quicker than a cobra and, on a fast break, Jesus, my stride was as long as a derby colt, and then on defense . . ."

Dawn would be coming soon, and light on the river, and I could almost see the Muncie Reds on the base paths, and Joe Nuxhall on the mound, and smell the hot dogs my father brought to me in the stands where I wanted to watch that clear, simple game go on and on and on, and never end.

It was a large stone beehive hut in the Aran Islands. One small rectangular entrance let the Irish monks into a dwelling as cold and unforgiving as the land that braced it. In black and white, the picture's theme was isolation from worldly cares and temptations, and I could imagine walking through bent grass and weeds on a rainy, foggy morning from the hard ground I had slept on toward sheer cliffs where only the turbulent sound of crashing waves disturbed the vast grayness of the world.

How could anyone live like that? I thought, staring at the page in a coffee-table version of a history of Ireland. In a moment, I supposed, Dr. Brown's receptionist would call me in for my final knee check, but I was in no hurry to leave the image of the bee hut and my old dream of a beekeeping hobby. I couldn't reconcile my memories of a swarm of bees with one bee going in and out of a hive. I wondered if the queen even did that.

I took the role of the bees, and I'm sure Dr. Brown thought I was crazy when I entered and left his office going *bzzzz, bzzzz, bzzzz*. But he gave my knees a clean bill of health, only reminding me that when I reached fifty I would have very serious arthritis problems.

I hadn't shot baskets for a month, and knowing that I could finally place behind me all thoughts of crutches, needles, locked knees, braces, and silver dollars, I headed toward the rims at the old Emerson school playground. The nets were new, the poles freshly painted, and the court had been blacktopped. But the trees, gravel, and swings around it were the same, and it didn't take much to revive a childlike energy. I ran some dashes and popped in some jump shots under the hot July sun, enjoying the squeaks and sweat and heavy breathing.

"You'll tear a knee or melt into a puddle doing it that hard."

I knew the voice, even before I turned to see Juanita, smiling and golden, swinging briskly with no hands on the chains.

"And you'll fall on your ass if you don't hold on," I said.

"Naw," she said. "I parachuted a couple of times last fall. This is a baby crib."

Not seeing a car or bicycle, I asked if she'd crawled out of hers to get here.

Juanita wiggled her feet in the air. "These," she said. She said she'd walked, out to Ball State, first, to check on her registration date, courses, and instructors for the fall term, and then, since my house was on the way back, she'd passed it. My mother was gardening, said I was down here, and why didn't I stop by to see you. "Must be that mind thing," I said. "I was going to call you tonight."

Her hair was shorter, and her smile had a slight curl at the corner, but it was as radiant as ever. She slid off the swing and stepped toward me. Juanita was taller, thinner, or maybe it was the shorter hair or yellow shorts and sweater or the way she reached out to slip the ball from my hand that made me think I couldn't quite connect the pictures of memory with the woman in front of me.

Her stroke was smooth, but the ball hit the underpart of the rim. "Better get a baton," I said, smiling wryly.

Her arched eyebrows and tighter lips said she didn't want to go back there, and I understood that for her, as for me, we would not segue into our past to recapture an old flame or an old condition. All right, I thought, we're starting today if we want to. I didn't know if I did. In fact, I didn't think I did. Juanita was as beautiful as any woman I would ever see, and as bright, charming, and fun. But I had learned to look ahead, at open space, and it wasn't monkish gray, or complicated by a history of distance and isolation. I couldn't see her in my future without looking back.

But when her smile returned, and playfully she began to march on the blacktop as I had done at Yopemika, I realized that she was as much a part of me as Chief Munsee was, and maybe in a kind of brief rush of association I could understand, too, what Bill Corrington and his South were about. You just can't deny where you come from or how you've lived. I was sure I could live without Juanita in the future, but not without the things she brought to me and brought out in me. Whoever I would love again would have to be part Juanita.

What we decided to do was have dinner, check out the Indian mounds at Anderson, drive out to the Muncie airport, stop by the Ball State library for a book on Civil War battles in Virginia, and one on wood finishing, and then rent a canoe. I agreed to go to a ballet performance at the Pittenger Center, and she agreed to go to *Cat on a Hot Tin Roof* and listen to my stories about Mississippi and New Orleans. She was working for a general practitioner most days until five o'clock, but we packed evenings and weekends with places to go. We both knew why. We wanted to have fun, not talk about us, and not get serious again.

It didn't work. Her hand touching my arm, if only once during the whole evening, is what I would remember most the next day. I thought about giving her a potted mushroom as a gift/joke, but decided on a small, colorful vase instead. She could put in it what she wanted. I would be selective in my going back. She swore she would not leave notes in the cuffs of my pants as she had once done. After two weeks, I found her fall sorority address, "In case you want to write," and couldn't recall where I had worn those trousers. She would be selective in looking ahead.

The silences got a little longer, and our stories of the past year eked out like shy but eager children. Perhaps we both shaded our tales so as not to hurt, or not to seem lost or lonely. We negotiated treacherous ground—going back to the past, but not to an emotional territory we had left. We wanted to be seen differently. I think we were surprised and relieved that reconnecting did not lead us back to a "quiet place," where we walled out the world. Our fortunes had changed very little, but our needs had.

It seemed that once we were past our tentativeness, past the groping *ifs* and *maybes,* we settled on the ground rules: no commitments, no plans for the future. The present was enough, because we had faced the past and found it would not hurt us. When Juanita said she felt independent and free, I understood it did not exclude me. When I spoke of consuming the geographical world, she did not feel left behind. Today, and as much of it as we could share together, was enough.

We carried on with trips—canoe trips, Saturday afternoon bike races through the county fairgrounds, meandering walks through favorite places.

The night she told me her mother was going to Indianapolis for the weekend, I suggested that, perhaps, we might have the apartment for ourselves. Partly a rueful dream, and partly a question, I wasn't sure how she would take it. I could tell she wasn't sure we were ready for that again. I had made love to Juanita, but we had never had a weekend entirely alone. Once in Kansas we'd stayed in a motel, but a late fraternity party and an early basketball practice left us clutching sleep more than each other. A curfew, deadline, hurried encounter, back seat, had always compressed our passion into a confined space, only explosive in its potential.

I asked her again later in the week about the weekend. She said I could come over Friday evening, and we'd see. I took that for a yes.

When she opened the screen door, I saw two mosquitoes slip in ahead of me. I shooed and chased, while Juanita laughed and wondered out loud what possessed me, they were only mosquitoes. I didn't want them on the walls watching, or landing on my butt as I was rising, or making that irritating sound close to my ear when I was listening to her breathing. They hid, and won, and for two days I periodically checked curtains and the tops of door jambs.

The music came first, Johnny Mathis most of the evening and "Twelfth of Never" over and over. Then we had veal parmigiana while we sat cross-legged on the front-room floor. She had cooked since forever, she said, but didn't like to on special occasions. Her mind needed to be uncluttered, unrecipeed. Maybe she should have tasted the sauce, though, she said; this needed a touch more garlic.

Looking at each other with bread in our mouths, we both realized this was delightful. We chewed in unison and tapped out glasses together. I think we let our eyes take their own time, because we wanted the adjustments in our own heads to settle, relax. We reached for each other's faces, hands, and, slowly, bodies. I asked if she would take off her sweater.

For the next two days, we traveled over territory that was never the same. The mole on Juanita's back had ever-changing contours. Her kneecaps revolved differently, and the left one was a centimeter larger. She delighted in a small scar she found on my inner thigh, and when she couldn't find it again claimed the large scar on my knee had eaten it. We put clothes on just to take them off. I cooked dinner while she commented on the different shapes of my butt as I moved from table to sink. She asked me quietly to hold the refrigerator door open longer as I stood in the light. We listened to each one pause, counted together the creaks in the box springs as we rose to climax, touched the braille of our hair. She swore she had seen my dream.

I think we fell back in love, but it did not have the feel of fixity about it. The rush of blood, or hungry emotion, or placid calm was linked with stages of our passion now, always flowing. Nothing seemed to stand still, or be deeper or more encompassing than this moment. We lived in the air where light and breath and touch were fleeting, and we reached again for what we'd just had. We knew no absences, no doors were closed, no intimacies unshared. We sought a oneness in space, not in time.

When the weekend was over, no line was drawn between that idyllic place and the traffic-filled streets of downtown. We took our world with us, and for the next fourteen days, one day at a time, we refined our sense of the present. We would consider Muncie a suburb of Baton Rouge, and live according to psychological rather than chronological time. We imagined a day in November. I would be taking a test at LSU in English 59. But we would be in each other's arms on page two. Then, on a lunch break at Ball State, she would rest her hand inside my shirt collar, while talking to a real estate agent about a property we wanted in Athens. There would be no walls in our world, an entirely feasible construction, when one understood the mysterious bond on which it rested. We had no sense of our bodies being apart. I jokingly pointed out to Juanita that we were, in fact, an actual manifestation of John Donne's poem, "A Valediction Forbidding Mourning":

> Our two souls therefore, which are one
>> Though I must go, endure not yet
> A breach, but an expansion,
>> Like gold to airy thinness beat.

She seriously said that she liked the fact of ether better; it was less fractional and more invasive than gold—but that, yes, gold was pretty, pretty things could be made out of gold.

I took a part-time job selling Kirby vacuum cleaners door to door, as I had previously done during some summer vacations, using the quick money to get back to school and carry me over until my athletic scholarship kicked in again. I worked afternoons, a few evenings, and saw Juanita less, but I had no sense of her absence. She was real to me when I needed her, in whatever mood, in whatever gesture I made—pouring salt out of a shaker or checking a rusty canister in my father's car. I knew it would be this way, whether I was in Muncie or not.

I think we had always thought of marriage as a condition rather than a state of being. My parents are married. One day we'll get married. These are the steps you take to get there, and then you're together forever. In a house. With children. That is what we imagined when we were pinned.

What we had now, we had no word for, and yet it seemed that all the stages had been completed, or didn't matter. The daily sense of struggles, uncertainties, doubts seemed tied to the future. Our future, where our feelings were concerned, was now. Therefore, I'm not sure why I wanted to confirm this state of wholeness. But I did. Even knowing that our previous pin-

ning had not worked while we were in college, I asked Juanita
if she would accept an engagement ring. Maybe it was, in fact, a
way of asking if all that I felt we now had was true for both of us.
I was certain, and maybe not. Juanita confirmed what I knew,
hoped, she would.

During the last week of August I began to finalize my trip
back to Baton Rouge once again. Tom and Marty were in town,
and Juanita and I spent several evenings with my family, cooking out, catching up. Preparing to enter law school in a couple
of weeks, Tom had returned from a summer camp where his
army reserve training had been accelerated by the conflict in
Lebanon. President Eisenhower had placed his unit on stand-
by, and Tom realized he might be called into war. He also realized, he said, that in two years of ROTC training, he had no
idea of how to lead men into battle. "I didn't know squat. I'd
never been tested. I had no idea how I would behave."

He said he immediately joined the airborne division to find
out what he was made of. For two months, Tom, the lieutenant,
was goaded, pushed, berated by a black sergeant, who demand-
ed obedience, perfect timing, unswerving courage. "He was
the best professional I ever worked with," Tom said, noting that
racial tension at Fort Benning, Georgia, made the sergeant's
job even more difficult. Some couldn't make the jump from the
fifty-foot tower, some froze at the exit from the airplane, one
guy landed on his own rifle, one landed on Tom's neck. At the
end, though, he understood what his sergeant meant when he
said, "I'd rather jump than eat."

Tom's unit was not called to Lebanon, but he had learned
what he wanted to know. He simply and quietly said, "I knew
what to do." I figured he would always quietly walk this earth,
knowing what to do.

I was packing the night before I was to leave, feeling that the
summer had turned out to be incredibly good, that this was the
way final farewells to youth should be. I was looking out my
back window, across the yard at the old walrus of a tree that
had weathered our winters and all of the basketballs banged
against its trunk. My mother called up that Juanita was on the
phone, crying.

I had a feeling.

My room would never be mine again. This house was now my parents' house only.

After I picked up the phone, I listened to Juanita crying softly for a few moments before she said,

"I'm pregnant. Dammit, I'm pregnant."

# 8

# Do Not Expect Too Much

The plaintive whistle of the Norfolk and Western southbound struck the dark night like the howling of a lost child. Maybe bored or signaling, the engineer eeked out a long wail that curled through the valley. I squinted out the coach window at the Great Smokies hovering all around us, and saw wavering shadows and my almost indistinct forehead reflected in the glass. Above the back seat in front of me, three pairs of faceless children's eyes, barely visible, stared without moving as my own eyes caught theirs. I closed mine, and listened to the clackety-clack of the wheels that in a few minutes evened out my breathing until I was no longer conscious of anything.

When Juanita stirred, I opened my eyes to the dim light of morning and the train slowing down. "Hammond," she said. "The last stop." Her voice was soft, her words almost whispering. She settled her head on my shoulder, tugged the blanket around her neck, and went back to sleep. I lay scrunched in the seat, watching the three pairs of eyes stare only at me. Shortly, I shouldered Juanita awake, and we briefly held each other like rag dolls tossed in a corner. We tried to smile, but couldn't. We never could get it back. The wedding night.

Instead we quietly gathered ourselves, our luggage, and moved through the aisle like members of a chain gang. I felt her pull the Just Married sticker from the back of my sport coat and stick it in the can in my pocket. The Purple Gang had nailed the can to my shoe with a short string. It rattled on the cement when we walked from Madison Street Church in Muncie to the train station. Thirteen hours between then and now.

"God, I'm thirsty," Juanita said, as we stepped onto the waiting dock of the depot in Hammond, Louisiana. A small jump, and a quick twirl around a woman with a baby and three children, and she was at the drinking fountain next to the entrance. As I was rearranging our two large bags and one hatbox, I heard a man say, "Not there, lady." I turned to see Juanita bending over the fountain to drink and a man in a business suit in the doorway, wagging his finger, and then pointing to a sign above her. She looked up at the "Colored Only" sign, then at the man, then drank deeply.

"Jesus Christ," the man said. "That's against the law, lady."

Juanita drank again. I stepped forward and asked the man if there was a problem. Gathering that the lady and I were together, and that wagging fingers at ladies was one thing, the man stepped down to the dock in a more appropriate manner for a confrontation with a man. "That's for niggers only," he said, pointing to the fountain, and pushing his chest closer to mine.

"Juanita," I said. "That water any good?"

"A bit lukewarm," she said, smiling. "It'll do. Good as anywhere."

I started toward the fountain, as a crowd began to gather. I didn't know what was next, but I was hoping no one would steal our luggage.

I heard Billy Flinn's voice behind me, and turned to see him holding our bags and gesturing frantically toward an open car door. Our team manager, who Coach McCreary said would pick us up, was desperately trying to urge us his way. I collected Juanita, and we walked back through the crowd. I expected to hear comments, zingy one-liners about Yankees or nigger lovers, but heard only a sullen, sweating silence stirring in the morning breeze.

I'm not sure why it was so easy to accept Juanita's quiet announcement of her pregnancy, since neither one of us ever expected a shotgun wedding. Obviously, we were not well informed or conscientious or fearful in our love-making. We thought, if we thought at all, that it could never happen to us. When it did, though feeling guilty and stupid, we began to plan our meetings with our parents, and our quickie exit. I know we felt a sense of violation, as though we had ravaged ourselves, disrupted a relationship that had none of this shame in it. But we did not imagine any other option than marriage. A few times before the wedding and after, I thought about my parents, my life, and even standing on a bridge over the Kaw River in Kansas, looking deeply into the deepest water. But the outside world had nothing to do with this blunder. We were not victims here.

We met separately with our parents. Juanita informed her father that she was getting married, and told her mother the truth of the circumstances. Her mother said she had thought I was a fine young man, and would still wait to see whether I was or not.

I could not gauge, at first, the degree of my parents' and brother's shock, except that its resonance was wordless. As we sat in the den, with its fine view of the rose trellis, they stared at me, as though they were still waiting to hear what I had said I wanted to talk about or were desperately trying to discover what they felt. I felt, ironically, more than at any other time, my specialness to them. Because I had betrayed it. Their evaluation of me, overall, I always knew, had been quite high. As I looked in their eyes, I saw it walk slowly down a hill.

Then, I thought for a moment that I was misreading. Maybe they were relieved or happy that my relationship with Juanita was settled. But my mother put an end to that.

"We like Juanita," she said. "We've always thought she was a lovely girl. I know you gave her a ring. But you've been so off and on. I'm sorry, I must ask this—are you sure the baby is yours?"

I knew the question had to be asked. It always was when young, intermittent affairs resulted in pregnancies. Along with others at parties, I had joked about it when several of my classmates joined the list of sexual incompetents.

"Yes, Mother," I said. "I am absolutely sure."

Maybe their relief began at this point. They knew now I was accepting responsibility, and their role was to support or reject. My mother began to cry softly. My brother nodded several times, and then patted my shoulder. When my father spoke, I knew he spoke for them all.

"You have disappointed us, son. This is very disappointing."

He began to walk around, stopping to look at family pictures on the wall, on top of the television. He pulled the curtains open a little wider, and stood in the light for a minute. He turned and asked my mother if that was all right.

"At the same time," he said. "We all feared this might happen. You have been infatuated with, in love with, Juanita since, I guess, you met her, so we worried you wouldn't give yourself time to grow, see the world, meet other women. We worried about that. We worry now that you'll be held back. We worry about that.

"But I guess we're confused. We thought we knew what you wanted. We always thought that, like Tom, you really wanted to get somewhere. You wanted to get more than we have. But we're worried now. You're in a minefield."

I remembered thinking, years ago, how the metaphors of war invaded many phases of our thought, and now I saw it ranged from basketball to love, as though each encounter was a measure of life or death. How could I tell my family that I was in no minefield? I would not be blown to bits before I could achieve what they wanted for me or I wanted for myself. Juanita and I had made a very human error, a very animal error, and we would adapt to our new environment with all the will and intelligence we could bring to it.

But I knew my father well. I knew where he would end. He would collectively worry for us all, then he would collectively judge for us all, and then he would collectively invoke all the spirits of hope and positive change that were in the universe.

"We will stand by you, son, and by Juanita, whether she remains here in Muncie or goes with you to Baton Rouge. You are starting your family when you're nineteen. Your mother and I started ours when we were thirty. We did the best we could, but, obviously, starting a family later in life doesn't make parents wiser or better teachers. We do know that somehow you'll get where you want to."

Good old positive Pop, I thought, recognizing that I had more doubts about where we were going, and with what, than he did.

As Milan was to Muncie, so Muncie was to Baton Rouge. This riverport and state capital of 160,000 had a commercial, political, and university complexion so intricate that a hand-shake on a golf course between a haberdasher and a senate staffer could influence the pedagogy in a history department classroom.

For over a century, the things that got done in the public sphere depended on an alliance. On the one hand were the entrenched power brokers—New Orleans families, north Louisiana landowners, oil and gas barons—who built and bought their way to a generational continuity. On the other was a rampant patronage political system, every governor's way of doing business. They were never far apart. Demon-driven, some thought. Heaven-sent, thought others. Massive amounts of unbudgeted money, the absence of regulatory laws and agencies, and adult cynicism and apathy, especially among the poor and black population, contributed to a climate of both corruption and reform that was self-serving. The "people" had no power, and even after the populist movement of the 1930s, the public agenda remained largely defined by the status quo.

It was no different in the late 1950s and early '60s when racial issues surfaced as a major public concern. While Alabama was dealing with the Montgomery bus boycott and Arkansas with the Little Rock school desegregation crisis, Baton Rouge leaders, state politicians, and university presidents and boards were constructing policies that would preserve segregation. A back-to-the-wall, form-barriers, them-vs.-us mentality prevailed in the alliance. When the issue of integration was raised on the LSU campus, as it was in June of 1958, it was immediately transformed by the state legislature into another issue. Sixty-six LSU faculty members signed a petition opposing legislative action that would close public schools ordered by the federal courts to integrate. The legislature responded by forming "The Joint Legislative Committee on Un-American Activities" to investigate the signers. The McCarthy era was alive in Louisiana, and the public debate over the merits of integration and segregation did not begin that fall.

The fall was devoted, almost exclusively, to one issue. Could the LSU football team really, could they actually, win the national championship?

Along with other young marrieds in our housing complex, Juanita and I enthusiastically joined the tailgate parties that started in the afternoon and ran until almost kick-off time. Then we would dash toward the cheap seats, the only ones we could afford, in the upper tier of the eighty-thousand-seat stadium. I would tell her to watch how quickly Warren Rabb dropped back, or Max Fugler plugged a line, or to keep an eye on the two guys in my "queer" story. During the Mississippi game, no one needed to explain anything to anyone as we watched Billy Cannon slip and slide, break six tackles, and run the length of the field. This was the year of the White Team, the Go Team, and the Chinese Bandits, an arrangement that allowed everyone on the roster to play offense or defense. Crowd favorites were widespread, fan commitments were deep. We even saw Berni Benstock and his new wife, Eve, and Pat Planchard and her new husband, Bob Prentiss, at one halftime, where we all marveled at what the summer had wrought.

At the height of the frenzy about football, the basketball team quietly began its season. Most followers expected another losing year, another rebuilding effort. But players dream, practice, get in shape, and read the papers closely only when they see their name. We had no reason to expect we would keep losing. Since I wouldn't play until the second semester, I ran wind sprints, shot goals alone, and played defense on the scrub unit. Coach McCreary drilled me on floor patterns, but kept me at the edge of pep talks. He insisted I eat lunch at the training table, instead of home. "You got to stay with the group, Phil. Stay tight with us." Neither Juanita nor I had a problem with that; one less meal to pay for.

With the generous help of our center, Joe Combs, and his wife, Juanita and I settled into a one-bedroom apartment, close to the university and close to an obstetrician's office, where she was hired as a receptionist. I had a scholarship that paid for books, tuition, fees, some housing and meals, but we often joked that we were no-wage and minimum-wage workers.

We didn't expect much. A walk on campus, a dance, a movie here and there, a couple over for hamburgers—that was all the time, or money, we had. Sitting on the back porch alone or on a blanket at the drill field, we would watch people flying kites, tossing every imaginable ball, ring, saucer, stick at each other and at leaping dogs. We would listen to the halting efforts of novice guitarists, and the wind shifted voices from open dorm windows. Children laughed, a long-distance runner huffed and puffed, and a carillon rang on schedule. That was enough. An inexpensive gumbo of pleasures.

At the end of the football season, undefeated LSU beat Mississippi State in a thriller, 7-6, and then thrashed Tulane 62-0. Even before they slipped by Clemson in the Sugar Bowl, the Tigers were declared national champions. Baton Rouge exploded, and January began with marching bands, even-handed praise, and buried hatchets. Governor Long, flanked by an entourage of protective deputies, declared that both he and God loved Louisiana above all things.

In the middle of January, I played my first game in an old, circular gym in New Orleans. On the bus ride to the Loyola University Field House, I realized I had been healing, scrimmaging, transferring, and practicing for two and a half years. I could feel the rust pocks in my skin clear to the bones. "Do not expect too much," I told myself, "and do not hurry this leadership thing." Nobody, not even myself, knew what I could do, and though Coach McCreary had touted me as one of his finest recruits, I knew I was taking a spot from a starter and joining a team that had an 8-7 record. What surprised me, as we neared the arena, was that I had been thinking mostly about Juanita, now six months pregnant, driving an old car with Joe's wife ninety miles to the game.

I think I could have been absent another five years, and still felt the same when I stepped on the floor. My ears went to particular sounds, and my eyes to the rim, the ball, knees and hands. Nothing else existed. I entered the zone where concentration is the only value. I felt fear and exhaustion during the game, but I thought them away. Time-outs and halftime were intrusions. Only once, during a foul shot, when I was taking a deep breath, did an alien thought invade: "I told you, you didn't have it!" Scotty's stepfather's phrase came from nowhere, and I missed the shot. I hammered my brain more tightly together.

I don't know whether or not it was a lingering euphoria over the LSU football season, but the *Morning Advocate* sports staff was aglow with our victory over Loyola. Its headline on the sports page read:

LSU DUMPS LOYOLA IN THRILLER, 70-68
* * * * * * * *
Phil Raisor Makes Tiger Cage
Debut with Winning Field Goal

I had had winning shots and headlines before, but that was long ago, and with the breakfast coffee, a hug from my wife, and a kiss on her belly for my growing child, I felt uncommonly content, even more to read that I would be able to play my game: "Many Tiger supporters were anxious to see Raisor in action. They were well-pleased with what they saw. The newcomer is fast and exhibits a bit of sleight-of-hand in passing off to other teammates. Occasionally, he used the between-the-leg pass and at other times flipped it from the back. All in all he should be a valuable asset to the Tigers as well as a crowd-pleaser."

I sent the article to my father, just to hear him on the phone, to hear him raving and dancing again.

After tentative gestures toward history and government, I decided to become an English major, a choice not unlike sliding in mud down a ravine—fun but dangerous. What do you do with an English degree? I was a college athlete, still dreaming of pro ball, but firmly rooted in a family tradition of practicality. If that doesn't work, then what? My brother was going to law school; I could follow. My father was a teacher and administrator, but I had seen his piles of paper, night after night. Foreign correspondent, big-game hunter, nightclub owner were no longer options.

By the time I was a junior, I was experienced enough with required and elective courses to gauge my abilities. Forget advanced trigonometry. Forget molecular biology. Literature, from various countries, captured my mind. I may have been drifting in that direction under Benstock's and the coterie's influence, but then, as a history major, writing a poem here, reading a novel there, seemed simply hobbies. When I found I *wanted* to write on literature more than any other subject, I flowed ineluctably home. But in your own home, poor as it may be, you want comfort. I realized that my attraction to literature was based on my desire to analyze, create, and conclude on my own. As long as I was not told that there was only one way of seeing, one interpretation, one set of variables, I remained challenged and inquisitive. I was not sure how I had gotten to this point of independence, and whether it was a good thing or not, but I was there.

If college was meaning anything to me, it was not in simply learning an organized body of knowledge. It was in watching the minds of my teachers, fellow students, and myself get from point A to—wherever. Although I found syllogistic reasoning interesting, I was more absorbed by associative thought, where connections and insights could be random, surprising, off-the-wall. Berni Benstock once told me to watch my mind work as I was talking, watch it work as I was listening to conversations. Keep an eye on how I thought, as much as what I thought.

So one day I stood with Juanita at the kitchen sink—my turn to wash, hers to dry—and watched our verbal and mental discussion.

"The baby kicked three times this afternoon, three hard wallops."

"Football or ballet kicks?" I asked.

Her eyes turned to a lump on the countertop. *Pork chop grease. Hardened. Need to get scouring powder. That's thirty cents. Tea, green beans, what else? What's he mean?*

"Both, I guess, but not if it's a she."

"Not if it's a he, either," I said. *A long field goal, then a pirouette? I don't think. Dear wife in football cleats? Fat and clumpy. Not Sylvia in Shakespeare class? Stretching and smiling. What would Lady Macbeth look like in . . .*

"Dr. St. Amant says I might have a difficult birth. Small hips." *What does he see when he looks down there? Stop. Big, I feel so big. I feel forks and spoons. Missed a spot. Say something. Something. Mother's joke.*

Berni laughed when he read what I had written.

"You're ready for *Ulysses*," he said. "You get to follow the minds of Stephen Dedalus, Leopold and Molly Bloom through a single day. Fully developed examples of stream of consciousness."

I was trying to impress Berni, so I didn't tell him I had read some of the Molly Bloom chapter before I wrote my little piece. I had gotten Joyce's novel from a used-book stall a month before, and then felt guilty for using part of the grocery money to buy it. I was beginning to find that scrimping induced characteristics of fawning and sneakiness. That did bring me closer to understanding Joyce's Dubliners and Faulkner's Snopes family, a set of characters I had thought earlier were simply stupid. Nonetheless, I decided poverty wasn't the best way to learn literature.

I began to believe I made the correct choice on a major later in the semester. I thought teachers just taught. Most teachers stood in the classroom, sat, or wandered around, producing from notes or memories information students should have. I was a good note taker. I had reams of notes—with plenty of blank spaces where I wandered off. But I now watched carefully their teaching process in the literature classes I took. I saw two distinct methods: an approach that separated literature from its social context, and an approach that placed literature in its cultural tradition: art-for-art's sake or art-for-the-world's sake. I was fascinated and tempted by each one. Oscar Wilde's *Picture of Dorian Gray,* which was all about form; or Émile Zola's *Nana,* which was all about life. Look at the beauty of this piece, or look at the painful death of this girl.

I took more notes in Dr. Waldo McNeir's class than anyone else's. He was a podium lecturer, a distributor of handouts, and a well-known Renaissance scholar. Tall, almost gangly, bespectacled, and rumpled, Dr. McNeir did the impossible. He lessened the obscurity of Spenser's difficult poem, *The Faerie Queene.* To McNeir, the Renaissance was not way back in the past. Its roots, ideas, heroes, and cowards were firmly entrenched in the present. Class after class we closely deciphered the work, attending to structure, rhythm, and image, while its characters—the Red Knight, Percival, Sir Guyon, the Queene herself—were connected to public figures in Spenser's own time. Then, in McNeir's world (and this didn't seem at all strange to me now), the poem became a contemporary work, still alive, revealing, meaningful. We knew he was an integration advocate, a leader of the statewide American Civil Liberties Union, but he did not press his political views. He wanted us to see that the issues in Spenser's poem could be understood in contemporary terms, that the issues were universal.

In a short period, I was as absorbed in my major as I was in basketball.

I did not see that I was drawing a curtain across myself. At night, after long practices, I studied hard at the library, only to get home after Juanita was asleep, or angered by my absence. I had never seen much of her anger, but its form was sullenness. She would stare at me, her body rigid and her breathing quite calm. I knew she was thinking, *Where have you been? Do you only think of yourself? I alone am bearing this child. Why can't you give me some of your time?* I would be penitent, responsive for a day or two, until we traveled to Georgia or Texas for games, and I would return, behind in my studies and determined to catch up.

I would change my pattern. I checked out the books at the library I would need, bring them home, and study in the bedroom. When she arrived from work, I had dinner ready, but then I would eat quickly, converse little, and retire to my studies.

I saw Juanita cry only once in Baton Rouge. In the middle of March, about two weeks away from delivery, I heard a hard thump against the bedroom door. I was eating a piece of toast on my way to class, and I stopped to listen. I heard a muffled, slightly moaning sound. When I opened the door, peeked in, I saw Juanita on a chair, her hands to her face. My presence brought an angry sob.

"What, honey? What is it?"

Juanita did not look up, or out of her hands, but said slowly, bitterly, "I could not put on my shoe. I could not reach down far enough to put on my shoe. I could not bring myself to ask for your help. Dammit, I did not feel you would give it to me."

Her hurt and rage, I now saw, was deep. I knew instinctively I could not hand her the shoe, or try to put it on, or apologize, or ask if there was anything I could do. I couldn't leave, but, then, I couldn't stay—until time had passed, this moment had passed, and I could return to rebuild a lost confidence. As I left,

I felt a rush of emotions overwhelm me. Once upon a time, I had let a fraternity pin drop from my hand. Once, I had held a letter that said good-bye. Now, I realized that for all of my studying, all of my reading about other's lives, and life, I hadn't grown a day older or wiser.

After the Loyola victory, the press and public, still aglow with a national championship, foresaw a rise in their basketball fortunes as well, the way a flooding river swells evenly over a long-resistant dam. Fellow students stopped in the cafeteria, and settled around me as though we were old friends. Football players at the training table called me by name. A half-dozen articles in the next week touted our chances for a strong revival in the Southeastern Conference. Our Loyola victory, my neighbor said, was an AP wire story, and appeared, he'd heard, in Los Angeles and New York papers. My father sent it to Coach Harp.

How far could we go? In spite of our next two close losses on the road to Mississippi State and Ole Miss, fan support remained strong. In a two-guard system, Dick Davies and I began to understand each other's moves, pauses, passing speeds. He was quick and flashy, too, so we could find each other in unexpected places, curling out of a pick or darting down the baseline. The radio announcers praised our team's speed and aggressiveness. We all knew we were undersized, and no matter how hard Joe Combs, Lynn Moon, and Jim Crisco banged the boards, larger front lines outrebounded us. Still, we gave the highly ranked Mississippi State team and their All-American center, Baily Howell, a scare before we lost by seven.

When we returned to play at the LSU Coliseum against Vanderbilt, the crowd had doubled. Actually, since the last three games had been on the road, our fans had not seen the *new* Bengal team play. Their imaginations, radio commentators, and sportswriters had been their eyes for over two weeks. No student cheering sections, no bands, no cheerleaders had been able to help us. They were ready now. Our warm-up drills elicited spontaneous shouts and pep songs. Tommy Raborn said his father had told him about fans in the rafters when Bob Pettit,

LSU's great All-American, played here. We looked up and laughed and hoped—someday. Let's start now.

Before we broke the huddle for the center jump, Coach McCreary told us that instead of our usual two-three pattern, he wanted us to run a one-three-one, with me in the middle instead of at point. "Let's shake 'em up," he said. "They won't expect this." I had never played in the middle, even in practice. Behind me, and on my back, would be a 6' 6" center. The first time I turned and twisted for a jump shot, he stuffed the ball in my forehead. I did not adjust well, and our front line, under this different system, only scored a total of fifteen points.

The *Advocate* newspaper story the next morning pointed out that "the Commodores dominated the backboards completely," and that we had scored only nine out of twenty-two field goal attempts. Without pointing fingers at coaches or players, it wondered if we knew our system as well as we should, seeming lost at times, and added that "newcomer Phil Raisor, bringing a 16-plus average into the game, got only five points and was erratic with his passing, although at times showing up as the kind of basketball player he is supposed to be—a first class one." Vanderbilt beat us by fifteen.

I had seen it before. In my senior year at Muncie Central. It is called the Loser's Syndrome. I'm sure it has been studied medically somewhere. Certainly, it is a condition well known to Sunday-morning quarterbacks, sports columnists, and alumni donors. What happens is that a team, with high expectations shattered, losing two games in a row, then four, maybe winning the next one, then losing two more, and then another, begins to separate like dead grass from green.

Here is how it goes. Play patterns are run aggressively, but not sharply. Coaches change starting lineups and systems. Players bicker or remain distant from each other. Fans show sympathy at first, anger second, offer solutions third, and disinterest fourth. Soon, practices lack energy. Road trips are long and silent. Clichés increase in the press room. Girlfriends or wives wonder what is wrong with you. You just want to be left alone.

I played in the last ten games of the season. We won only three. The Losing Syndrome set in for all of us after we lost, in sequence, to Georgia Tech, Alabama, and Auburn. By the end of the season, we had all learned to sit on the bench one game, not play, and then be in the starting lineup for the next one. I was surprised to hear a month later that I had been picked by the Associated Press as one of "the best playmakers in the Southeastern Conference." Small solace for me, and an irritation to others, who had learned that my impact on LSU fortunes was a small one.

Once again, or I should say still, I raised the issue of recruiting with Coach McCreary, but he was in no mood now to tolerate my suggestions. Clearly, he was disappointed with our season and, I think, with me as a player. I am sure that when he recruited me, he expected me to lead this team into his imagined territory. Another guard, he said, from Bossier City and a 6' 10" player from New Orleans were on his priority list. He said I would have to accept the fact that this was Louisiana, and segregation was the policy of the university; in fact it was the law of the state. "Let's get on with reality, Phil," he said. "Let's go with what we can."

I now sensed in Coach McCreary what I had sensed in Coach Harp. For whatever reasons, I hadn't fulfilled their expectations. Maybe it was my playing, maybe it was my attitude. Coach McCreary knew me as a basketball player better than anyone, but what worked at Muncie Central to motivate me no longer did. Shouting, periodic benchings, and simply expecting respect for the man and his coaching record would not turn me or the program around. The rest of the country was entering a new era in athletics and life, and we were mired in losing, racism, and Old South politics. I tried, for the only time in my life, to talk to Coach McCreary about failure, but he pointed out that the LSU football team had just won the national championship with its tradition still entrenched.

After my transfer from Kansas, I actually had two more years on my athletic scholarship. We began the next season as we ended the last one. By midpoint in the year, the record was three wins, nine losses. We had constant lineup shifts, increasing distance from players and staff, and serious rumblings about hiring a new coach.

Perhaps in despair, Coach McCreary started four sophomores against nationally ranked Kentucky to another disastrous end. He kicked Joe Borgini, our rebound leader, off the team for incessant grumbling. George Nattin suffered an ankle injury. At the end of a game against Mississippi State in Starksville, the crowd rioted, swarmed onto the floor, and battered us against the walls. Joe Clune was smashed by a State football player, swallowed his tongue, and turning purple, writhed on the floor until Billy Flinn extracted it. Our season was like that—writhing on the floor.

When the season ended, I decided to forgo my last year of eligibility, complete my degree over the summer, and enter graduate school in the fall. I applied for a teaching assistantship in LSU's English department and was granted one. Coach McCreary and I had one final conversation. It was frank and momentarily painful. His parting counsel to me was, "Get out of the books sometimes, and have some fun." Surprising, I thought, since we'd never talked about either. But we did end by reminiscing about better times. That is the way it should have ended, I think.

I don't know what "coaching" is, having chosen a different career, but contrary to what Dr. Naismith said, ironically perhaps—that coaches don't matter—I think coaches are essential to young people, even in their failures. From my perspective, as a player, I knew at eight years old, playing on gravel courts, that winning was good, losing bad. I learned early, the learning coming mainly from repetition, that rules, fundamentals, and training are required to play basketball. I also discovered that bruises, arguments, resentments, and teamwork come naturally with the territory. What I needed a coach for was to fit me into a vision and make my role clear and meaningful to me. I don't mean a vision of patterns or tempo or tactics. I mean a vision of basketball.

I thought of myself as a student/athlete, and I needed a coach who would talk to me about the history, lore, dangers, social importance and, yes, even whether basketball was all about winning or an experience that should help us understand the human spirit. I needed to understand the significance of losing, how to use it to win. I got x's and o's from Coaches McCreary and Harp and not an education. I don't know. Maybe I would have been more successful with them, played harder for them,

if they had known what I needed. But that would have required
seeing me, seeing all of us, not just as a team, a group, but as
distinct individuals. That would have also required the skill to
talk about subjects other than basketball in order to be talking
about basketball.

I know that my fifteen years in this sport, from its joyful
beginning to its melancholy end, could be viewed differently—
as the story of a promising but undeveloped athlete, or a player who couldn't fit in, or a young man in the wrong place at the
wrong time, or one who didn't make it to the NBA, or one who
didn't drop out and got his degree. Or, in fact, about one who
learned on his own more about winning from losing than the
other way around.

But, in a sense, I've never finished playing. I know what
every athlete knows, that game day is only part of the game.
A ripped-down rebound, a twisting dribble down the floor, a
last-second jump shot that rims in or out, or an elbow stuck in
a lazy forward's ribs doesn't define us. Neither does the won-
and-lost record. What defines us is what we bring to the game
on either a winning or losing team. We all know the perpetual-
motion enthusiasm of a second-string guard on a 4-25 team,
as well as the whining, selfish superstar on a 25-0 front-runner.
Both seem oblivious to the real circumstance, like the news-
caster reading about a midair explosion over Honduras with a
canned smile on his face. But that's what they bring, who they
are, on or off the court. Whether we like it or not, we bring our
whole lives to a team, to a game, and the more we understand
about ourselves the better we (and coaches) can gauge our
contributions. That seems true to me even now. I'm still trying
to keep a winning spirit from losing.

Bill Corrington returned to LSU in the fall as an instructor,
with his new wife and master's degree in hand. Joyce Corrington
was a lovely, vibrant scientist who was an intellectual match
for Bill. Discussions in their apartment kitchen ranged widely
and wildly from Gnosticism through Beat poetry to molecular
orbital theory. Down-to-earth as well, both Bill and Joyce were
comedians and earthy storytellers. Contesting the air and
ambience in Berni and Eve Benstock's kitchen were odors of

gazpacho, Ise-Ebi Tempura, and chocolate potato cakes. Both excellent home chefs, Berni and Eve postered their walls with lithographs and Picasso prints, exhibited contemporary sculpture, and scattered Arabian rugs on their floors. Cushioned and dimly lit, their apartment was a learned study, where laughter was brisk and infectious, and usually connected to food, literature, art, film, and international travel.

Both the Corringtons and Benstocks were young professionals, and Juanita and I, though younger and students, were treated as friends. We learned about faculty life that way, and I'm sure my decision two years later to apply for a teaching position was strongly influenced by their world, which seemed, to us, intellectually sophisticated, creative, family oriented, socially committed, and economically sound. By the time I started teaching, though, Juanita and I had two children, with Jon Bradford on the way. Our early years of faculty life were spent in kitchens full of diapers, pot pies, and paint peeling off the walls.

I met Billy Mills in the Corrington's kitchen. He and Bill had been undergraduates together at Centenary College in Shreveport. After a stint in the army, Billy started his graduate work at the same time I did. He was deceptively country, with an accent of a good ol' boy and a slippery bargaining manner that made me want to keep my hand on my back pocket. I was to learn that he had many voices, and many manners, and could change as naturally and easily as a chameleon.

"Hell, yes," he said. "I know this boy. He played basketball here. I don't know whether you were any good or not, but, say, did I tell you I knew Billy Cannon. I don't mean I knew him, because he was behind me, but I played on the same team with Jimmy Taylor in junior high school, so we were ahead of Billy, and Jimmy went on to play for the Green Bay Packers. That was here in Baton Rouge, and do you know, oh, this is a good one, you gonna owe me a drink for this one. I heard Billy Cannon got busted for robbery in high school and as part of his probation had to get permission to leave the state to play football games, and, uh, oh, there's a potpourri of stories about them athlete lads."

"And what?" I managed to get in, while Corrington and I just sat back smiling.

"Oh, this is good," Billy said, his hands twisting the air, and his rapid speech running like a halfback through his periodic "uh's" and "oh's." "You jocks are something. I mean, you guys—there's a bar down about two blocks from North Street, downtown, the Boulevard Bar, and that's where the homosexuals go, where they hang out, and the word was that some of the football players used to go down there and, shall I say, entice them out to the levee. And, oh, yeah, then they'd take their money and beat the shit out of them.

"Now this is what I heard. I'm sayin' the hearsay. One of these guys was an LSU professor, and he knew who one of the players was and brought him up on charges, and there you see, that's one more time when the gladiators got eaten by the tiger. Do you see the irony of that—the tiger. LSU Tigers. Now isn't that something."

Yes, I thought that was something. It's a small world, was all I could think. It seemed that maybe those at Kellog's party "for me" were practiced executioners. I shook my head, laughing, and told him I certainly would buy him a drink, but not at the Boulevard Bar. Billy Mills and I formed a friendship, where his agile mind made it possible to jump from sports to literature to politics to women to wherever we wanted to go.

We took several classes together, and one of them was Dr. McNeir's graduate seminar, a course that covered works other than *The Faerie Queene*. Billy's quirky speech and enthusiastic manner delighted both Dr. McNeir and the rest of the class. At times, though, Billy would pause, slow down, and deliver an interpretation of "Colin Clout Comes Home Again" or "The Sonnets" that would clamp the parts of the poems together and roll them out like a finished product. We felt that we had just gotten a gift.

One afternoon, as we sat at the Three Coins Inn, a continental pub and restaurant, reading local papers and some of the owner's newspaper imports, Billy muttered, "Oh, shit. Shit has hit the fan. Read this." He handed me a section of the *Advocate* and pointed to a letter that was being reprinted:

November 14, 1960

Representative Wellborn Jack
House of Representatives
State Capitol
Baton Rouge, La.

Dear Representative Jack:

I disagree with everything you stand for. Segregation is wrong. Interposition is of no legal force. State sovereignty is a dead doctrine. This state of Louisiana is no more than one of fifty states making up the federal union. It is elementary that the U.S. Supreme Court is empowered to interpret the Constitution of the United States. We must live under the rule of federal law or perish. Reason must prevail.

Sincerely yours,
Waldo F. McNeir

I didn't know who Wellborn Jack was, but Billy said Waldo McNeir was crazy to take on that man. "He'd eat possum raw, and wash it down with swamp water."

I saw, with Billy, that a big issue was shaping up between the legislature and the university, another incident compounding an already festering conflict. I felt closer to it now, more mentally and emotionally involved than in 1958, when the Louisiana "McCarthy" committee was formed. Later, Berni acknowledged that he had been one of the sixty-six faculty members who had opposed the legislature's proposals to close public schools rather than to integrate them. He assumed he was still under investigation.

After we left the Three Coins, Billy stopped on the street outside and began slowly to revolve on his heels looking around at Main Street, up at the buildings, and down to the white porticos of the state capitol, as though he were taking in a bag full of memories. "McNeir's got some guts," Billy said. "More damn guts than maggots on a dead squirrel." I assumed that was a nod in the direction of praise, but it might have been touched with irony as well.

When I was saw Bill Corrington the next day, he was shaking his head.

"The man wrote his letter on LSU stationery," he said. "My, God. He's an idiot. They'll kill him."

"What makes the difference?" I asked. His look was like the one he'd given me a long time ago when I didn't know anything about Pickett's charge.

"Official stationery," he said slowly. "They'll say he's speaking for the university, that he's disrespectful to his employers, that he's not acting in a professorial manner."

"What if he hadn't used it?" I asked, expecting to see that look again.

Bill just dropped his head. "Then," he said, "Waldo would have been an individual citizen, with all the rights of a citizen to call his legislator any damn fool thing he wanted to."

"You mean they'll split the hair that fine, over stationery?" I asked.

"With a serrated knife," Bill said, and slid his hand across his throat. Then he said a strange thing. "I hope it's not the kind of mistake Lieutenant Raisor would make."

"Who's he when he's not at home?" I asked.

Bill smiled and said, "Listen, I want to use your name in my novel."

I knew Bill was writing a novel about the Civil War, from a southern perspective. He'd told me he was calling it *And Wait for the Night* and would be finished next year or so. I was flattered, and said sure, who was this Lieutenant? Bill told me he was a young Yankee, and not to worry because he was the best damn Yankee in the book. My relief was momentary because, upon reflection, I knew how he felt about Yankees in general and most of us in particular. I saw that he was enjoying this, and he only very slowly pulled a manuscript from his desk and read:

As Raisor pushed against the wagon, the mules heaved forward. His hands slipped on the smooth wet wood and he fell, full-length, into the churned dark gruel beneath.

—Lootenant, lemme help you.

—It's all right, Raisor said, wiping his hands on the back of his breeches, trying to scrape the mud from his eyes.—I'm all right.

But he was not all right. Wave after wave of nausea swept over him. The slaughter, the rain, the long road riddled with pits and holes—and the screams of a man with an ounce of flattened lead riding in his belly.

Bill closed the book as slowly as he'd opened it.

"You leave me there," I asked, "in the mud?"

"Down in the mud," he said. "Down where the southern boys are, down with the disenfranchised, tossed away, wounded Negroes. Down where you start to learn something worth learning."

I deduced that he was developing a coming-of-age character. In the end, the Lieutenant would probably get to see some of Corrington's light. I also knew, though, he had no idea what I meant, walking away, when I muttered under my breath, "First I'm down in the mud with pigs in the North, and have to learn something. Then I'm down in the mud with southern boys and blacks in the South, and have to learn something. Either I've got to learn to be a pig and stay in, or learn to be a man and get out. Choices, always the damn choices."

# 9

# Under Court Order

An unusual snowstorm hit Baton Rouge overnight like a Mississippi River flood, and as I stepped off the side porch of our apartment on Cloverdale, I thought I was in Indiana. I tucked the petitions in the manila folder inside my jacket and began shuffling and scooping my way through the yard snow toward the street. I knew that neither snow plows nor salt would get to us today, so only pedestrians and a few cars would make channels in this stuff. Zero-degree air had made the top of the snow crusty, and the crunching sound I made as I nudged forward, mixed with the periodic crack and thump of a falling limb, were the only punctures of a frozen silence. Birds were hunkered down as I crossed between the two lakes onto Dalrymple. As I got closer to the university, the task got easier. Foot and car traffic made paths on West Lake Shore Drive. When I got to the largely residential LSU campus, I was met by snowmen, snow angels, igloos, and gangs of students pelting each other, and then me, with snowballs. Shouts and laughter rose steadily as I darted and ducked toward the Field House to meet Billy for the big event.

The day before, we had worked all afternoon at the Unicorn on the petition. It took shape slowly. Billy and I agreed on the principal thrust of the protest. Academic freedom was the primary issue. But how to frame it, how to phrase it, what to include as subcategories—that we debated and negotiated.

"Hell, Phil, this can't be about segregation. You know that. We're white, but they'd still hang us—that is, after they'd hacked off our balls."

"Well, we don't have any balls if we don't get it in there. McNeir made it *the* issue. We're saying that as a professor, he should have the right to his opinion, whether anybody agrees with it or not. Academic freedom. But that doesn't mean we can't go after Welborn Jack, Senator Rainach, and even President Middleton."

"You want to lose that teaching assistantship don't you? Juanita'll kick your ass."

"Hell, Billy. We're English majors, wordsmiths. We can get it in there."

"All right. All right. Let me work on it, partner," Billy said. "But no names, not this time. We'll take it slow. You wanna tree the coon 'fore you got a gun. Let's see if we got any support out there first."

We finished the final draft as snow began to fall and spent an hour at the library duplicating copies. On the way to the Three Coins for a drink and a strategy session, Billy, rolling a snow-ball in his hand, began telling me about the snow in Japan and Korea, and the women, and his job with the Army Security Agency. It all sounded so mysterious—the secret rendezvous, flashing signals, packages dropped on roadsides, the path through the mountain, and one who didn't come back. He snooped on double agents. Nothing was clear, but nothing was vague either. Maybe I dreamed he was an undercover agent, or maybe it was the way he told the story, but to this day, world traveler that he is, I still think he's an operative of some kind.

When he heard later that, after we left the Unicorn, two men asked the owner all sorts of questions about us, took notes, and said he might not want to associate with us, Billy chuckled, "What fool's running their show? Damn that's so obvious." He said he would not be surprised to hear that our names were in the final report filed by the Louisiana "Joint Legislative Committee on Un-American Activities." At the moment, I was brave. I said I hoped so.

The LSU president and World War II hero, Troy H. Middleton, was unambiguous in establishing his position on segregation. He told his Board of Supervisors that

Louisiana State University has repeatedly made it clear it does not want Negro students. Like several other of the State's institutions of higher learning, it admits them under court order. They attend LSU through no fault on the part of the University which to date has done more than any institution, organization or individual to try to preserve segregation in Louisiana.

But since the 1958 faculty petition, Middleton had been under steady pressure from the legislature to purge LSU of any creeping integrationist sentiment. In turn, he urged his board and the faculty to support him in his efforts to forestall a legislative intrusion into university business. The Joint Committee hovered for two years, but after public distribution of the McNeir letters, it pounced on Middleton. In turn, Middleton pounced on McNeir.

McNeir was advised that an ad hoc presidential committee would hear charges against him, and his dismissal was possible. In class, Billy and I heard Waldo McNeir say that he had simply spoken as an individual and had the right to do so. He smiled and winked at me as I left. "See?" he said. *The Faerie Queene* is still very much alive."

I stopped by his office after class. His hand was shaking as he talked to his wife on the phone. When he hung up, he slumped back in his chair and said, "My public self and my private self aren't always the same. I must admit, I'm a bit scared." He was scared that his eleven years at LSU and his work with the Louisiana Civil Liberties Union might end. He was scared that if the university could fire him, that if the tenure system didn't work, his colleagues would retreat into fear and trembling. "Because I used university stationery, they say. All right. I shouldn't have, but that's what I had at the time. It's all a ruse anyway. If not this, they'd find some other reason to get me. But Middleton, my God, he's going to cave in. I swear he is!"

I began to see a student protest forming in my mind, a collection of signatures like the faculty one, students rising in support of free speech, faculty and students together in support of LSU, a new LSU, open and free to explore any subject, to recruit from anywhere, to be a model for the South. When I told Dr. McNeir what I saw, he smiled first, then said slowly, "You'll want to be careful, son. Just a few years ago, in 1955, we had two black graduate students, properly registered, taking classes, who were beaten and shot on campus. We've got people who will do that here, son. You must be careful."

I was careful not to fall on my butt as I walked past the Greek Theater, and scooted along the driveway in front of the Field House cafeteria. I knew that if I went flying, the petitions might exit my jacket like scattering bees. Billy had probably danced his own version of a sliding mannequin on his way to the front door, but he was there now and laughing at me. He said I was late, and I said I was not, and he said school had been canceled, and I said it had not, and he said he was having hot, hot coffee first, and I agreed that was a good idea.

I don't know how many students were in classes, but clearly most of them were either sliding and sledding outside or sipping hot, hot coffee in the packed cafeteria. We couldn't even find a place to sit down, so we didn't. We sipped and divided the room into zones, realizing that we now had the problem of mass congestion. We could be separated, lose sight of each other, duplicate our efforts, and miss many of the milling students. Also, we could not help each other if necessary.

"Look," Billy said. "Let's try it this way first. You keep your petitions in your jacket, and just follow behind me. I'll keep moving, and you see what happens to the ones I hand out. See if anybody's signing them. See if they get moved around." Billy stepped into another one of his skins, another set of his eyes. He became sharply focused and rigid, as he calculated where he would enter and where he would exit. His hand, inadvertently it seemed, slipped to his belt, and then he bent to check his ankle. Then he shook his head at himself, and relaxed back to his usual, slightly paunchy posture.

I followed him in. Levity and easy informality were going to be his approach.

"Got some ol' homemade red eye here I'd like you to taste. Thank you."

"Passin' these out to pay for some overdue books at the library. Thank you. Please pass 'em on."

"This here'll warm your hands, and your boyfriend's heart there. Sign it if you will. Thank you."

Billy stepped deftly over piles of books, around students squatting, and in between different small groups laughing, bending, gesturing. He'd slip a petition into a hand of a talking student, nod, "When you get a chance," he'd say, and move on.

One girl with wide-rimmed glasses and straight hair pointed to a word, and mouthed *misspelled*. Taken aback, Billy looked hard, and then, slightly smiling, mouthed *No, that's correct*. She turned away, shaking her head vigorously. I saw one girl sign, and watched a boy erase it. Two students read the petition, and then began debating each other.

In the center of the cafeteria, where people were sitting at tables, Billy moved quickly as though he'd entered a valley from a dense forest. He didn't stop to explain or argue or convince. Dropping off two petitions at each table, he covered the section in five minutes. It began to quiet down as people read.

"Bulllllshiiit," a young man groaned, and the room turned toward him.

"This is a bunch of crap," another one said more slowly, as though he was surprised to find it in his hands.

The afternoon before, Juanita had said what was true and predictable. Anger will come first, and then the personal resentment. For many students, LSU was a safe haven. Few blacks on campus, none at social events, no troubling discussions allowed in the classrooms over segregation, no integrationist stump speeches permitted to disturb the ancient oaks and magnolias in the courtyard. Segregation and free speech were not major issues, were they, when right thinking and right conduct prevailed among so many?

When I told Juanita what I wanted to do at the Field House, not sure whether I was asking for her support or permission, she lifted our daughter, Staci Lynn, off her lap, and handed her to me. I pulled her close, smelling the blanket, the powder, and touched the sleeping eyes, as though they were soft fur. It seemed as though Juanita and I, alienated at times, could hold Staci for awhile and quietly return to each other.

In the spring, when our daughter was born, my mother said she had to be there. She couldn't stay away, and took her in her arms as soon as she could. "Staci Lynn. Staci, you call her. Staci has your brother's light hair and complexion, but look at those eyes. Your eyes, Phil." I asked what she meant. "You both look straight ahead like you see the world half full." I smiled. "Or half completed, Mother," I said.

Two weeks later, after diaper changes and laughing in the

kitchen and late-night talks, my mother, holding Juanita's hand, said good-bye at the train station. "You have a wonderful family," she said. "Juanita is perfect for you." As we were walking away from the baggage car, Juanita nudged me. "Remember," she said. "Mothers know best."

Juanita was looking out the window at the snow beginning to fall when I returned from putting Staci to bed.

"I don't think it will stick," I said.

"By morning," she said, "you'll wish you had a dog sled to get you to your Field House."

"What do you think?" I asked.

"I think you'll have to decide, and let me know."

"I know," I said. "But I just wanted your opinion."

"My opinion is that you have a wife, a daughter, another child on the way, a poor-paying teaching fellowship, four pot pies, six eggs, and a half gallon of milk in the refrigerator, a year left on your master's, and a Yankee heritage in a southern cesspool you know nothing about. You don't belong in the middle of this. Billy does."

"I don't think it matters where I'm from," I said.

"Tell that to Bill Corrington and Berni. Both care about you greatly, and they're glad you want what they want. But Bill wants it led by southerners, and Berni wants it part of a worldwide revolution. You get stomping around at that Field House with your petitions, and you'll sink, my darling."

I walked behind her to hold her. Knowing that she wouldn't be at the Field House, where neither of us wanted her, I said lightly, "You would save me, though, wouldn't you?"

She turned before I could wrap my arms around her.

"Oh, Phil," she said. "I grew up poor, from a broken home broken up twice, separated from a mother's and father's affection all my life, unable ever to have a real home, unable to finish my college degree, isolated from my husband's thoughts most of the time, plagued by migraines, surrounded by people who want me to be contented.

"I'm not contented. I have things I want to do, to achieve. My dreams for me didn't stop when we got married. They didn't stop with this child. I want you both in my life, and I'm not going anywhere. But this is my mind and my body. I give them to both of you. But I keep them, too."

I stepped back, feeling as though air had been pulled from around me. "Does that mean you don't love me enough to save me?"

She smiled, shook her head slowly, and came into my arms. "It's not about love, darling," she said. "It's about saving yourself."

In the silence, as we held each other, I let her words sink in. Slowly I felt the rightness of them. They seemed true to her life. How else had she learned to survive, to live, to relate to others, without drowning? I suddenly thought of what my mother had once said about having to save yourself. I didn't know my mother's life. I couldn't understand. I knew Juanita's life. I felt closer to her now than ever before.

I slipped into the crowd on the right side of the cafeteria, and began handing out petitions. Word spread, and those without copies reached for them. Fingers, shoulders, parkas, twisting and turning in front of me, and my own heart-thumping energy, made me slightly dizzy. I think the bumps I received were accidental, but I began to hear on my side of the room mumbled dismay.

Nothing had yet materialized that made me see danger, but body language and scraping chairs, and my own sense of a festering uneasiness, made me certain everyone expected a disruption. As I reached the inner circle, I saw Billy slowly working his way toward me, sliding between tables, collecting a petition here and there, easing past an arm thrust across his chest. One student we knew from McNeir's class stepped quietly on top of a chair, mimicked tying a rope around his neck, and then contorted his face and arms as though he were hanging. One girl in front of me started to cry. I wasn't sure if it was because of the mimicry or released tension.

The cafeteria went silent. I handed out a few more petitions, then felt the waves of bodies behind fall away and divide. I turned to see a few, and then a few more, LSU letter jackets moving toward me. My mind darted to an assemblage of letter jackets braced on a fence rail over looking a pig sty. Below us, the aliens that didn't matter, creatures unlike us, who we need give no thought to or those who cared for them. Now, I felt stuck in mud, awaiting an assault. The body in front of me took a petition from my hand, and I watched it move to a table and step up on it.

"Listen to this shit," it said and began to read, mockingly,

*There comes a time when we as LSU students feel we must express collectively our deep concern with events which cast shadows over our quest for knowledge and the democratic principles this nation is founded on. One recent event which we all know about endangers our freedom to express an opinion.*

*Without reservation, we oppose the actions of our Legislators in their determination to ferret out professors of this university who speak freely their own minds. This is not a matter of segregation or integration; that issue is yet to be debated on this campus. But we cannot continue to be a great university if we don't allow faculty, students, administrators, and staff to speak plainly and openly. We implore the Legislature to listen to the people, and let us speak our minds.*

*Below, we have transfixed our names, having no desire to hide, through these difficult times, in a cloak of anonymity.*

The petition, raised in the air, was very slowly torn in half. It separated in two hands, which slowly moved away from each other, and let the shorn pieces drift toward the floor. I heard the voice from the table top say: "Now that is freedom of expression."

The laughter in the room broke not the tension, but the containment of restrained words. Chatter resumed, applause followed, and the figure stepped to the floor. I saw who it was, and, looking behind me, who they were.

I was facing about twelve or thirteen LSU football players.

I recognized six or seven, and they recognized me. I had only been away from the training table for part of a semester, and I had played golf with several of them. I'd tutored one on a sociology paper, until he told me he just wanted me to write it. No hard feelings, he said, when I bowed out. Around the athletes, as with most other students, I relaxed, and joked, and got along. We all had our opinions. Mine seemed radical to many, but I didn't push them. That was good enough for most people, except those who had heard from somebody who had heard from somebody else that I was this or that they didn't like.

Petitions were still in my hand. I stepped back, and handed a student one, asking if she would sign it when she had time. I saw it tweaked from her hand and torn in half.

"You want to do anything about that, Raisor?"

He had spoken his piece on top of the table, but he wasn't finished. I had known him to be a dangerous halfback, small and quick, with a lethal dart through the front line. He'd nod to me at the training table but not much more. I remembered cheering for him from the stands when we wanted him in the lineup. Now, his face was close to mine, his breath smelling of eggs and bacon.

I turned and walked a few steps away, handing out another petition to a wide-eyed young man who hesitated to take it, looking back over my shoulder, but also feeling the pressure of my gesture. He took it, and stepped back.

We both saw the arm of a letter jacket pass by me, into the boy's hand, click the paper from him, and another face pressed close to mine.

"You want to do anything about that, you Commie?" he said, as he tore up the petition.

Again I knew who this one was. He was a massive second- or third-string all-conference tackle or guard, who had a great, infectious laugh. I once sat at a bar with him and listened to him talk about his love of opera and his desire one day to sing, if only in his hometown. He gave me a one-note demonstration, startling me with my glass halfway to my mouth, and then he broke into hiccuping laughter.

I barely reached out with the next petition, when it was ripped up in my face.

"You want to do anything about that, you Yankee son-of-a-bitch? And you know somethin', Raisor? I just don't like your looks." My golf buddy this time. He wanted to smash my face just as Wayne Klepfer had done. Wayne's image rose momentarily. He was as large as ever. I couldn't yet see a minister in this Wayne nor the beating up on himself it would take to get him there. But, still, I saw him differently. I didn't need to bust him. I didn't need to run from him.

Billy made his way to my side, but I told him to stay back. This was personal. I had no intention of diving headlong into a Wayne Klepfer or a half dozen two-hundred-plus-pound men who, at the present moment, wanted my head and throat in their hands and fists. I saw in their faces that this game was life, a war, not a pastime or sport, but a battle in the trenches, blood and guts, victory at all costs. They had taken all their high-school years, their families' and fans' support, their mental and physical training for fifteen years and made it their world. It was a world that could not be seen differently and could not be changed.

But their game was not my game. I had learned much from Milan.

"You want to do anything about that, you nigger-loving queer?"

I saw the knuckles of a fist close to my nose, and then grind slowly across my chin, as it pulled down and ripped another petition in my face. Now I was a "nigger-loving queer," and I knew who had said it. I could have told him that he had an ugly butt and that his pirouette was clumsy, but I smiled just enough to let him know I knew who he was, that quickly turning off a red light and padding into another room did not allow him to ride anonymously into the night.

I was now the worst of all enemies. None of them had ever played against black players in high school or college games in Louisiana. State law forbid it "in order to protect the public health and morals, and provide better education and promote good order in the state." Blacks were always on the other side of things, everything, and they could be kept in their place, couldn't they? But a white man, speaking up, that was a worse danger because someone might listen, and, someday, who knows when, God forbid, the walls might come tumbling down. Think of your daughter, think of who might be in the legislature one day. Not if I can stop it! And the faces of those who stared into my face, who did not care about a petition or a professor, cared very much about shutting down Billy and me.

But I was more than they knew. I was in a hotel hallway in Indianapolis, and outside a restaurant in downtown Muncie. I looked into Oscar Robertson's eyes. I was on a street in Detroit.

Only a few months had passed since my father sent the clipping. John Casterlow dead at twenty-three. September 7, 1960. I saw him step quickly from the driver's side of his car, lurch into the three men bad-mouthing his wife. The knife wasn't flashed, wasn't even shown. It came deep in our chest. Our legs crumbled. Crawling up, a hand on a jacket, another sharp pain in the side, "You mother . . . ," all six-foot-six falling again, down, into a jack-booted toe, into a tire iron coming down again and again, and his wife screaming, and our hands clutching the air for one more chance at them.

And I couldn't get you off that cement, and out of that blood, and where you never should have been, not there, but here, saying, "Hand this one to them, Phil. Take and hand this one to them. Here, I'll do it."

"This is for John Casterlow," he said. "Please sign it."

"This is for John Casterlow," I said. "Please sign it."

"This is for John Casterlow," he said. "Sign the son-of-a-bitch."

I kept passing out the petitions, hearing them ripped, feeling the bumps and elbows becoming more aggressive. I would pass them out until they were gone, and then, if possible, Billy and I would collect some, and walk quietly and firmly from the building. But I also thought, just sit down, stay right here, let them bring in the campus police, the water hoses, don't be dislodged from this act.

Out of the corner of my eye, I saw Billy step up on a chair, lumbering slowly with an easy smile on his face.

"Now, look y'all, we just asking you to think. That's all. Just to think a little." His palms were open, and his gestures were even and relaxed. I know some in the back could not hear because he kept his voice conversational. "I don't want us all here thinking we've got some kind of revolution going on in our state of Louisiana. I am not interested in radical change. Hell, my hero's still Robert E. Lee. My daddy was born in Mississippi. I was born in Baton Rouge. I figure any problems we got we can take care of right here among us. But the state's telling us we can't talk. Now, I know the legislature's afraid we want to talk about integration, and that's why they want to shut us up. I, personally, want to talk about the crime rate going up because not enough of our tax dollars are going to the police, and I also want to talk about our tax dollars. I, uh, want some of them back. And I want to talk about the federal government's intrusion into our schools, and the state government's intrusion into who I go to a party with. I want to talk about why we don't have more plays on campus, and, yes, why President Middleton wants to fire Professor McNeir. See, I want to talk about a lot of things, and some of them you may be interested in, and some you may not. And, oh, I bet you got a peck of things you don't want anybody telling you how to think about, even your parents. When you go home on vacation I bet you have your say. You're an adult now, and Mommy and Daddy don't have to think for you, tell you to shut up.

"Well, we're just asking you to say to our legislature, don't tell us to shut up. That's all. That's all we're doing. Don't tell us to shut up."

Even the football players looked at each other. I saw students glancing down at the petition, reading quickly what they had already read, and a few nodded. A few were pointing to words, a few looked up at Billy and then toward the football players. One girl turned to me and said,

"You take out that crap about segregation and integration in there, and I'll sign it." I heard myself say no to myself, but not to her. Billy had gone his direction, and it was working.

"Now listen everybody to what she's asking. She's asking us to take out that sentence about the debate on integration and segregation not starting here yet. You see that, about halfway down."

Billy looked at me from his roost. I was still surrounded by football players who were puzzled, not I think at what he was saying, but at the shift in momentum; a sneaky play had been called from the sidelines. Billy was telling me he saw where he wanted to go. I nodded.

"I'll tell you what you do. If you don't want it in there, you just cross a line through it. You just take a pencil or pen and cross through it. Then, you sign it. And you see, that's what we're talking about, that's free speech. You agree with what you agree with, and don't with what you don't, and you don't want to be shut up about it."

Then Billy looked at me, and decided he'd better say something else.

"And you know," he said, "if you want it left in there, then you can leave it, and sign it, and that's *still* free speech. You can do that too. We've got enough copies here we can do it that way."

Billy stepped down, and a few signed petitions were handed to him, and then a few were passed to me, and then we collected some with both hands. Nobody was laughing or showing relief; they were talking among themselves as they drifted back to their seats or out of the cafeteria. The wind was blowing in from outside, and somebody yelled to shut the damn door.

One football player stopped about a golf club away from me and stared. He was the son of a well-known segregationist who was widely respected among corporate and university leaders. I remember wildly applauding his single-minded guttiness to take the big hits and bounce right back up into the next murderous charge.

"Watch your back, Raisor," he said. "From now on, you better watch your fucking back."

I did watch my back, and the backs of my wife and children, for the next year and a half, but not from a hole, nor peeking around walls. Billy and I sent our signed petitions, over eighty of them, to the capitol, and the faculty had its own quiet campaign that gathered 117 signatures. Their petition also addressed academic freedom, and the activities of the Joint Committee as well: "We recognize the right of the legislature and duty of the legislature to conduct investigations of the University. When, however, its actions curtail freedom of expression or create an atmosphere of fear, it does a great disservice to the University and to the state which it serves."

In the spring, President Middleton threatened to dismiss Waldo McNeir for violating university and professional standards. Charged with introducing controversial subjects into his classes that were not relevant to English literature and with using university stationery to convey his private opinions, Professor McNeir chose to resign, telling the *Morning Advocate,* "By their continuing efforts to curtail the academic freedom of the

University, the legislature has degraded LSU in the eyes of the nation," and that he "was glad to go to a more democratic section of the country where professors are not censured for exercising their rights as American citizens." Texas was not far away, but Dr. McNeir and the University of Houston felt he would fit in fine there.

I could neither understand nor accept Dr. McNeir's treatment, either socially or intellectually. He was a southerner, whose tempered and organized approach toward controversial issues would have allowed for open discussions on the LSU campus. As an issue, race was introduced in his Renaissance course when the white Desdemona in Shakespeare's *Othello* was married to a black general. "This is a love story," McNeir said. "And we need to understand the Renaissance view of love. Also, how do we view love today? Does our view affect how we see this relationship? Should it?" The class was hesitant, with only a few of us talking, but only those who wanted no discussion of race at all, no matter how relevant to the work or world, were upset. After Dr. McNeir left LSU, I knew that, as a teacher, I would enter a literary work on the side of art for art's sake, but not leave it alone until it was connected to the world's sake.

Billy and I watched staunch resistance and fear wrap the campus in its own insulated cocoon. Even sympathetic faculty cautioned us against further demonstrations. A column in the *Daily Reveille,* the campus newspaper, which had offered several challenging, thoughtful editorials on academic freedom and race a year earlier, now resorted to old stereotypes: "To say that the basic right to life is denied the Negro is to deny the fact that more of them are alive in the South than anywhere else in the nation. If one wishes to see a real demonstration of liberty and pursuit of happiness he has only to prowl the Negro sections of any Southern city or town after dark. Semantic argument could be raised as to how much 'happiness' one sees, but these quarters are undeniably the scenes of the most unfettered pursuit of happiness possible within the framework of civilization."

But real-life Negroes, in the spring of 1960, were starting to sit at lunch counters in Kress's, Sitman's drugstore, and the Greyhound bus station. They would be told they were breaking the law, they weren't wanted, they should go back to Africa. From the campus of Southern University, an all-black state college twelve miles from LSU, the students trickled, then swarmed, into Baton Rouge. Against the advice of their president and many of their parents, a half-dozen leaders organized sit-ins, marches, and boycotts, which for a month rattled the whole fabric of Louisiana society.

Freedom rides began in the South in the summer, and Medgar Evers and three young men were killed in Mississippi three years later, but the revolution, which began elsewhere, had already come to Louisiana's state capital. I could stand on the edge of it, now in the aisles behind those who ordered coffee. If they were not served, if they sat in terror, the movement, I was told, was theirs. For now, my help wasn't needed. Their black arms on the countertops is what they wanted the world to see.

For the first time, I thought I understood what John Casterlow and Oscar Robertson saw when the two basketball adversaries shook hands at the end of a game. Color did matter. Maybe it would not forever, but for now, it was a bond that only they, at the deepest level, could share. How could that not be true? My wife's bond with herself was rooted in the same perception. We don't choose our circumstances, but we certainly rise or fall on what and who we learn to trust. If she trusted herself more than me, she was right to do so. She had learned from long experience that she would not let herself down. I was still learning.

We all were.

During our last month in Baton Rouge, I received a phone call from my father asking if I knew about the story. What story? I asked. He didn't know, but he'd just heard from a bookstore in Muncie that my name was in a new release titled *Best College Writing, 1961*. Did I know about it? Was that me?

The national *Story Magazine* contest. I yelled "Yes, it's me!" and began dancing around the kitchen. My daughter thought it was fun and danced with me. We swirled into the front room, picked up Brent, my new son, out of his crib, and spun onto the porch. I yelled "It's published!" and we spiraled into the yard and back toward the kitchen. Juanita was hanging up laundry and watching as though she was afraid of my energy, worried about her children, but pleased.

"What brought that on?" she yelled from under a large sheet.

"I thought it was lost. Never got there. I didn't know," I yelled back.

"I don't get it. What are you talking about?"

"It won!" I shouted. "I won!"

As soon as I said it, Juanita's head abruptly appeared and her hands lifted toward her question. "You were in another game?"

Yes, there I was, in another game.

Juanita came to us with towel in hand. She put her head inside our faces and breathed deeply. We all smelled of perfume and sweat and freshly washed hair and wet diaper. I knew I would say something to her about the richness of all this, of her at the center of our small constellation, but I had nothing formed yet. It would end up, "I love you," and maybe that would be enough for her.

But not for me. I would need to understand what I really meant. By now, abstractions were possible for me if I lived them. I knew I had come more easily to fear than love, as though I was naturally inclined to games where I had to win or lose. But love couldn't be about that. I knew now that all these years I'd been both fox running for his dinner and rabbit running for his life. I'd adapted enough to survive somewhat on my own terms, and I'd regained a balance that let me walk upright. But love couldn't be about that.

Juanita turned back to the clothesline, leaving me with two fidgety children in my arms, and a towel to hang up. Her going made me think that someday love might leave with her, pack its bags and find its way to a less scrupulous spirit who would simply let it be what it was. I knew I should be content with the moment, and let my right hand guide the tricycle and my left hold the bottle. But I wondered now that I loved so deeply, how I could hold on to it even if Juanita left, my family broke up, I lost my calling, or like Holden Caulfield and Sgt. Croft the whole world turned against me. How could I hold on to it until the game was over, and even after?

But love couldn't be about that.

It would be years before I would understand that I was in a

distinct genetic line of lovers. None of us in the family doubts that the thunder that rocked our first conscious ancestors taught them to love those who were as vulnerable as they were. Terror and love are not separate for us. We know they were born in the same moment. That's why we embody a little of the chicken that's afraid of hawks when it hatches and the rat that learns in the lab to skirt the shock. Some of the clan will walk thirteen flights to avoid riding the elevator that terrifies them. Then, when the door opens, they step in to hold a child in their arms.

But sometimes we're bold. We put things together that other breeds say don't belong. We merge imaginations and emotions, countries and races. We even change the physical landscape. Cartographers claim that the White River, Kaw River, and Mississippi River do not intersect. In my own experience they do. I know the problem is simply one of perception. Some of us look underground, where all waters seep out of their channels and creep blindly and inevitably toward new connections. I know I followed those rivers from Muncie to Kansas to Louisiana and discovered a geography of love and fear not seen by others who traveled before me.

Simply stated, we take the outside world inside and make it our own. Then we're responsible for what we do in it.

I understood my roots only after I had gone back into my hole to find out what had happened there. I had grown up in a walled-in city that walled out danger, and was barely conscious of a world outside when I was forced to face the porousness of walls. A sudden blow in adolescence awakened me to the fact that I didn't own anything, not even myself. I spent years afraid of being nothing. In time, I would learn I was a grab-bag of old wounds, generous sentiments, crowning achievements, defeats that begin inside, and all the other signatures I would collect in my fluid world.

I salvage everything now. John Casterlow's bushwacking, Juanita's pride, Wilt Chamberlain's devastating loss, both Wayne Klepfer's fist and his transformation into minister are mine as much as theirs. In the end, I suppose, I don't control much, but I do look everywhere I can and hold onto the dream that someday my eyes will see what my imagination offers.

But on this day, while flapping a towel and hearing my daughter's laughter, I had a brief glimpse of a consoling future. Even a thousand years from now, when Juanita is green or blue and I am the color of warped wood, our children will play basketball on a coral reef, and listen to old fish tales about the Milan-Muncie game. Fred Scott and Billy Mills will join Senator McCarthy in a round-up of squid under a Lebanese oil tanker, and Coach Harp will return as a northern pike. Then we'll change in the next millenium.

A circus act, a mirage, you might say. That world is impossible. But I look at it this way. Milan took the expected future—that they would lose to a more powerful team—and imagined another one. Losers, it seems to me, are those who too readily accept the conventional wisdom, whatever it is. If the natural world is taking billions of years to tell its story, then if we choose to be here, we ought to believe we can write our own.

Juanita returned with a tubful of clothes, talking some nonsense about sharing duties. I agreed and told her where the lawn mower was. We didn't need to laugh. We just touched long enough to be sure we saw each other, and then she handed me another towel to hang on the line.

# Acknowledgments

Juanita, in 2001, ended her thirty-year career at the *Virginian-Pilot*. As both a journalist and homemaker, she brought intelligence, intensity, and humor to both worlds. She remains at the center of my universe. Juanita did not always recall the events of this story as I did, but her care in reading the drafts of *Outside Shooter,* and our sometimes painful discussions, just remembering, getting the facts correct, brought it closer to the truth of our memories.

I am especially grateful to Michael Pearson, whose nonfiction works and critique of the manuscript were both guides and models of painstaking I admire. Reservations about an early draft by my longtime colleagues and friends, Karl Knight and David Shores, made me think harder. Comments by Philip Gerard, Erin McGraw, Ronald L. Speer, and Joe Cosco were insightful and encouraging.

I would also like to thank the archival and special collections staff at Louisiana State University's Hill Memorial Library, and particularly to Mary Herbert Price, the director of Oral History, whose doctoral dissertation on the Civil Rights movement in Baton Rouge remains that period's most comprehensive study.

Grateful acknowledgment is also made to Marian Blue and Celeste Mergens, editors of an anthology, *Sea of Voices, Isle of Story* (Triple Tree Press), who published in 2003 an excerpt from chapter two of *Outside Shooter.*

# About the Author

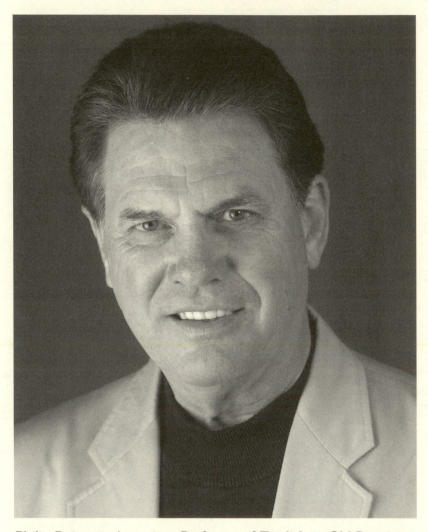

Philip Raisor is Associate Professor of English at Old Dominion University in Norfolk, Virginia. He is the editor of *Tuned and Under Tension: The Recent Poetry of W. D. Snodgrass.*